At Issue

Intelligent Design
Versus Evolution

Other Books in the At Issue Series:

At Issue

Intelligent Design Versus Evolution

Louise Gerdes, Book Editor

GREENHAVEN PRESS

An imprint of Thomson Gale, a part of The Thomson Corporation

Detroit • New York • San Francisco • New Haven, Conn. • Waterville, Maine • London

Christine Nasso, *Publisher*
Elizabeth Des Chenes, *Managing Editor*

© 2008 The Gale Group.

Star logo is a trademark and Gale and Greenhaven Press are registered trademarks used herein under license.

For more information, contact:
Greenhaven Press
27500 Drake Rd.
Farmington Hills, MI 48331-3535
Or you can visit our Internet site at http://www.gale.com

ISBN-13: 978-0-7377-3679-3 (hardcover)
ISBN-10: 0-7377-3679-8 (hardcover)
ISBN-13: 978-07377-3680-9 (pbk.)
ISBN-10: 0-7377-3680-1 (pbk.)

Library of Congress Control Number: 2007938126

Contents

Introduction

In 2005 the Kansas Board of Education revised the definition of science in its science-teaching standards. While the new definition retained the concept that science is about observing, measuring, and testing hypotheses, it rejected the idea that science is a search for "natural" explanations of human life and origins and opened the door to explore "supernatural" explanations in its classrooms. Under the new definition, biology teachers would be required to discuss alternative theories to evolution. One such theory is intelligent design—the idea that life is so complex that it could only have been created by an intelligent being. Many scientists argue that intelligent design (ID) theory is simply disguised creationism, a movement to prohibit the teaching of evolution in public schools. Intelligent design advocates dispute this claim, arguing that attempts to conflate intelligent design and creationism are unwarranted.

Consideration of the history of the controversy is useful to understand the conflict between the science and intelligent design communities. Long before Charles Darwin published his evolutionary theory in *Origin of Species* (1859), those who studied nature were called natural philosophers, not scientists. Scholars did not specialize in a specific area of study such as theology or biology. Indeed, one of the purposes of studying natural phenomena was to learn about God. The modern scientific method—the gathering of observable, measurable evidence, the formulation of hypotheses, and experimentation— did not develop until the scientific revolution, which reached its height during the sixteenth and early seventeenth centuries. Not until the early nineteenth century, did scholars in Europe and the United States change their approach and the direction of scientific inquiry. Scientists, as natural philosophers came to call themselves, agreed that they should not introduce supernatural explanations for natural phenomena. While they believed that God made the rules that guided nature, they wanted to understand the rules of nature without drawing conclusions based upon their religious faith.

Darwin's evolutionary theory was developed using this new approach. Although many Christian leaders believed Darwin's theory to be wrong because it contradicted the Bible, the scientific community, which now saw science as an area of study distinct from theology, embraced the theory. By the twentieth century, most scientists accepted natural selection as a key biological fact. The world was changing, however, and some blamed what they saw as a decline in morality on the philosophy of materialism, the idea that everything, including thoughts and feelings, could be explained in terms of material, physical phenomena. Creationists believed that attributing human behavior and thinking to the principle of natural selection was corrupting society; a return to Biblical principles, they believed, would save it.

Thus in the early 1920s, William Jennings Bryan led a campaign to outlaw the teaching of evolution. Indeed nine state legislatures banned or limited teaching the theory. In 1925 biology teacher John Scopes was convicted of violating Tennessee's law prohibiting the teaching of evolution in the famed courtroom battle between Bryan and legendary lawyer Clarence Darrow. Tennessee's law forbade the teaching of "any theory that denies the story of the Divine Creation of man as taught in the Bible, and [teaches] instead that man has descended from a lower order of animals." When challenged about the law's constitutionality—its violation of the First Amendment clause that forbids the government from establishing a religion—Bryan responded, "What shall it profit a man. . . if he shall gain all the learning of the school and lose his faith in God?" For decades to follow creationists, also known as Biblical literalists, led successful campaigns nationwide that banned the teaching of evolution in public schools.

Some commentators claim that the cold war led to a shift in American attitudes. The threat posed by Soviet technology focused U.S. attention on the importance of a sound math and science education, and schools began to include evolution in their science curriculum. In 1968, in *Epperson v. Arkansas*, the U.S. Supreme Court invalidated an Arkansas statute that prohibited the teaching of evolution in public schools and universities. As science grew in importance in the minds of Americans, however, so did the strategy of creationists, whose new goal was to prove the scientific accuracy of Biblical creation. Institutes were founded and books were published to support "creation science." Law student Wendell Bird suggested in 1978 that failing to allow the teaching of scientific creationism violated the First Amendment rights of Biblical literalists, and some states approved bills that prohibited the teaching of evolution unless creation science was also taught. In 1987 the U.S. Supreme Court declared such laws unconstitutional in *Edwards v. Aguilard*. However, Justice Antonin Scalia's dissenting opinion argued that criticism of evolution should be taught in school, which some suggest opened the door for the new creationism—intelligent design.

Commentators who claim that intelligent design is creationism in disguise argue that like creationism, intelligent design calls upon a supernatural force to explain the origin of life. This, they argue, is theology, not science. According to ID critic Justin Gero, "ID invokes an unseen force to explain the origin of life. The second that ID supporters invoke the supernatural to explain anything." Gero argues: "it is no longer science. Science cannot observe or test the supernatural. That is a philosophical and theological idea." Intelligent design supporters dispute this claim and deny any connection to theology. "Unlike creationism, the scientific theory of intelligent design is agnostic regarding the source of design and has no commitment to defending Genesis, the Bible or any other sacred text," claims ID advocate John G. West. William A. Dembski, author of *The Design Inference*, agrees: "The most obvious difference is that scientific creationism has prior religious commitments whereas intelligent design does not. . . . Intelligent design . . . has no prior religious commitments and interprets the data of science on generally accepted scientific principles."

Those who believe these counterclaims are insufficient to distinguish intelligent design from creationism respond that ID theorists have failed to produce scientific evidence to support the theory. The National Academy of Sciences maintains, "Creationism, intelligent design and other claims of supernatural intervention in the origin of life or of species are not science because they are not testable by the methods of science." The Intelligent Design and Evolution Awareness (IDEA) Center answers that "ID proponents have submitted their ides to mainstream journals only to see them turned down. This is because of the immense bias faced by ID proponents in getting their ideas published." Despite this bias, the IDEA Center reveals, Dembski has published extensive work grounding his critique of neo-Darwinism in empirical arguments. "Intelligent design theory," the Center argues, "is based upon these empirical arguments."

Whether intelligent design is creationism in disguise or a legitimate scientific theory remains controversial. In February 2007 the Kansas Board of Education again adopted new science standards, this time returning to mainstream scientific views of evolution. However, the battle is not likely over as the divergent viewpoints in *At Issue: Intelligent Design Versus Evolution* make clear.

1

The Intelligent Design Versus Evolution Debate: An Overview

Neil Munro

Neil Munro writes on issues of science and technology for the National Journal, *a weekly magazine on politics and government.*

The intelligent-design (ID) and evolution controversy is a debate between those who oppose scientific materialism, a belief system that ID advocates claim ignores moral concerns and religious values, and scientists defending years of scientific accomplishments. ID proponents claim that the theory of evolution does not explain complex processes and that public schools should teach that an intelligent designer could fill these gaps. Scientists argue that no scientific evidence supports the existence of an intelligent designer. Teaching ID, scientists fear, will confuse students because it erroneously paints science as anti-God and hostile to American values.

There's been a lot of media coverage recently [as of 2006] about "intelligent design" versus the arguments for or against Charles Darwin's theory of evolution. This coverage has often treated the dispute as a boxing match between religion and science, between faith and data, as if either were somehow capable of knocking out the other in six rounds. But the dispute is also part of an enduring political fight, in

Neil Munro, "Evolution on Trial—Debating Design," *National Journal*, vol. 38, January 7, 2006. pp. 36–43. Copyright 2007 by National Journal Group Inc. Reprinted with permission from National Journal. All rights reserved.

which the strongest partisans of rival philosophies argue that their beliefs are better for the country and for democracy.

The clash plays out in newspapers, in magazines, and on television—but in recent years, most sharply at the meetings of local school boards, where elected members set policies for grades K-12 science education. At those meetings, advocacy groups and allied parents present cacophonous arguments— some scientific, some political, some constitutional—to sway the curriculum decisions in their favor.

The ID Movement

Today's debates are fueled by the intelligent-design movement, whose core advocates and their allies argue that the variety and complexity of life on Earth is too sophisticated to have evolved randomly, and must have been guided by some form of unseen intelligent hand.

Intelligent-design advocates have a clear political goal, albeit one that is inextricably linked to their religious perspectives. That goal is to lessen the political clout of "scientific materialism," which is the idea that everything that needs explaining—including life, free will, and morality—can be explained solely by the predictable and pitiless interactions of matter as it seeks to organize and selfishly proliferate itself. In the starkest version of this view, long-standing notions of the human spirit and of divine intervention are merely outmoded attempts to impose order on a cold universe and to govern humanity's restless appetites. The intelligent-design camp asserts that pushing back materialism will open up more room for moral claims and religious arguments in the political arena.

To accomplish this goal, intelligent-design advocates are trying to undermine the main pillar of materialism: Darwin's theory of evolution, which was first published in 1859. Evolution is central to materialism because it offers a comprehensive explanation of how humanity emerged from lower creatures rather than from supernatural creation. This theory has provided the intellectual foundation for the assertion that the origins of life are material, not divine.

To undermine the authority of evolution, intelligent-design advocates publish what they say are scientific critiques of evolution, highlight what they call deleterious political consequences of the theory's ascendance, and press school boards to include criticisms of evolution in school curriculum.

Intelligent-design backers . . . insist that their main target is not science per se, but rather the scientific arguments for evolution and the attendant notion of materialism.

Intelligent design's attack on materialism is a challenge to scientists because materialism is as central to science as clearly marked ballots are to election results. So scientists are fighting back, and contending that intelligent-design advocates are new-age "creationists" who are pitching a politically tailored pseudoscience that is, and should be, constitutionally barred from taxpayer-funded schools.

Science's Impact on Politics

It's hard to buck science. Scientific advances, almost anyone would agree, have had a vast and positive impact on society. Progress in science has helped treat disease, create products that make life easier and more enjoyable, and generate great wealth. In 1850 in America, 217 of every 1,000 infants died in their first year of life; in 2000, fewer than six babies in 1,000 died before their first birthday. Without that improvement in survival rate, parents would be burying roughly 800,000 of the 4 million infants born in the United States every year.

America's economic growth is also tied in no small part to advances in science and technology. In 1929, the U.S. gross domestic product was equivalent to $865 billion, measured in

2000 dollars. By 2005, GDP had multiplied fourteenfold, to $12 trillion, much to the delight of Americans, both religious and irreligious.

Today, most people view scientists and their findings as authoritative. Indeed, many argue that religion's authority has been diminished, or at least put on the defensive, ever since the Scopes trial in 1925. John Scopes, a high school biology teacher in Tennessee, was prosecuted that year for teaching evolution. He was found guilty, but the state Supreme Court dismissed his case on a technicality, thus preventing an appeal to the U.S. Supreme Court.

Although the Scopes trial was a legal victory for the creationists of the day, it was a cultural defeat. The anti-Darwin campaign fizzled out, and religious conservatives retreated from national politics while urban technocrats, scientists, and university-trained experts increasingly gained economic, political, and cultural clout. Religious activists finally returned to politics in 1980, and they have since revived the conservative influence on politics and culture.

Evolution's Ill Effects

Creationists, as distinct from intelligent-design advocates, cite Bible passages about Adam and Eve, their descendants, and Noah's ark to explain the origins of humanity, to set the Earth's age between 6,000 and 10,000 years, and even to explain the death of the dinosaurs. In contrast, intelligent-design adherents accept the basic process of evolution, but say that the process had intelligent help along the way. And they try to use scientific arguments to make their case, in a tacit recognition of science's usefulness and enormous political clout.

Their principal argument is that nature's complexity, such as the anatomy of the human eye or the multistep chemical process that coagulates blood, cannot be fundamentally explained by material causes, random mutations, and the "survival of the fittest" doctrine, as evolution theory says.

Intelligent-design advocates assert, for example, that the biology of blood clotting could not have evolved piece by piece, because it doesn't work unless all of the necessary mechanisms and proteins are present. These theorists say that something else is needed to explain the origin of mankind, biological complexity, and other "loose ends" of evolution, and that something else is "intelligent design."

Their claim is far-reaching, yet quite narrow. Intelligent-design proponents generally do not deny the geological evidence that the Earth is 4.5 billion years old, and they agree that creatures and plants evolve. On paper, most intelligent-design advocates don't argue that the intelligent designer is God, and they even leave open the possibility that the Earth could have been designed by aliens.

Moreover, advocates say that K-12 students should not be taught that an "intelligent designer" exists, but only that evolution's "loose ends" might be explained by the existence of an as-yet-undiscovered intelligent designer. That's the position of John West, the associate director of the wellspring for intelligent-design supporters, the Discovery Institute's Center for Science and Culture, based in Seattle. The center receives money from a variety of foundations, many of them allied with Christian conservatives.

Intelligent-design supporters are presenting their case to a nation in which creationism is already a mainstream belief.

Ideology or Science?

The intelligent-design camp says its pitch is scientific, although scientists widely disagree. Intelligent-design backers also insist that their main target is not science *per se*, but rather the scientific arguments for evolution and the attendant notion of materialism, which they see as more of a political movement, and a dangerous one at that. "Our biggest beef is that we don't think students are learning enough about" evolution, West said. "It is being taught like an ideology, not a scientific theory."

West argues that Darwin's emphasis on the material origins of humanity is perilous and dehumanizing. It was embraced, he says, by political advocates promoting fascism and communism in the early 20th century and was also important in the influence of Social Darwinism in the United States during the 1920s and 1930s. . . .

John West and his followers fear that such notions will shape public attitudes and spill over into politics. "This [materialist] mind-set—that you can reduce everything to either a chemical reaction or to genes—is very dehumanizing," West said. "It does really conflict with the idea of human free will and free choice."

Intelligent Design's Political Progress

In their political campaign against the materialist view of humanity, West and his allies have a few advantages.

For one, voters do not have to choose between evolution or religious faith. They can freely support government-funded biomedical research and also choose to think of themselves as the holders of inalienable, self-evident political rights endowed by a creator. By downplaying possible inconsistencies, people can simultaneously get their therapies, distance society from a materialist nature, and champion a set of legal rights and moral rules to govern themselves and their fellow citizens. Lark Myers, a middle-aged shop owner in Dover, Pa., told the *Washington Post* [in 2005], for example, that "I definitely would prefer to believe that God created me, than that I'm 50th cousin to a silverback ape."

Second, intelligent-design supporters are presenting their case to a nation in which creationism is already a mainstream belief. In a November 2004 poll of 885 Americans, of whom

795 were registered voters, 55 percent said they believe God created man and woman in their present form, and 27 percent said God guided the evolutionary process. Only 13 percent—barely one in eight—agreed with the statement, "Humans evolved, God did not guide the process," according to the poll, which was conducted for CBS News and the *New York Times*.

Practically all leading scientists oppose the intelligent-design argument, root and branch.

The same poll, however, suggests that most Americans are willing to play both sides of the fence: Only 37 percent of respondents—18 percent less than the number who identified themselves as creationists—said they wanted schools to teach creationism in place of evolution, while 65 percent said that schools should teach both creationism and evolution. . . .

Mixed Success

Overall, the intelligent-design crowd has had uneven success. They haven't dented scientists' support of evolution, and they haven't yet, as they have promised, carried out peer-reviewed scientific experiments to prove their case. And so far [as of January 2006], no court that has considered a case involving intelligent design has approved teaching the idea in K-12 classes.

Scientists assert that apart from the deleterious effects of intelligent design on classroom teaching, and on the scientific community itself, the theory is, well, bunk.

Nonetheless, intelligent-design advocates have made great progress in winning over like-minded social conservatives, in presenting their case to the public, in getting their ideas recognized by a few school boards, and in garnering support from leading political and religious figures. [In July 2005], the

New York Times ran an op-ed article by Catholic Cardinal Christoph Schonborn of Vienna, who reasserted the claim that faith is compatible with evolution and with intelligent design. "Evolution in the sense of common ancestry might be true, but evolution in the neo-Darwinian sense—an unguided, unplanned process of random variation and natural selection—is not," he wrote. "Any system of thought that denies or seeks to explain away the overwhelming evidence for design in biology is ideology, not science."

In August [2005], President [George W.] Bush declared that local school boards should decided how to deal with the intelligent-design claim and that "part of education is to expose people to different schools of thought." Sen. Rick Santorum, R-Pa., echoed the president's call for diversity in education when be said in August that teachers "should lay out areas in which the evidence supports evolution and the areas in the evidence that do not," although he also said, "I'm not comfortable with intelligent design being taught [as recognized truth] in the science classroom."

The Scientists' Response

Practically all leading scientists oppose the intelligent-design argument, root and branch. And it is hard to overstate how strongly they hold to their own argument that acceptance of intelligent design could undermine generations of accomplishment achieved by the scientific method of rigorous testing and retesting of hypotheses. This doesn't mean that scientists reject God or religion. "The intelligent-design movement has the potential to drive a wedge between people in the United States—and especially young people in schools—and the whole idea of science ... by portraying science as anti-God, hostile to American values, and close-minded on evolution," said Kenneth Miller, a biology professor at Brown University and a practicing Catholic who actively campaigns against intelligent design. If that happens, "science as a career, and science as a way of thinking, and America's unique hospitality to science . . . will all be put in jeopardy." But expecting people who have spent their lifetimes finding out how the world works to accept an untested hypothesis brought forward by a conservative think tank and its allies, and to support its dissemination in the nation's schools, is implausible.

Politicians are already trying to drive a wedge between scientists and public policy, Miller said. . . . "I think it is happening on a significant scale right now," Miller said.

The worries about intelligent design go far beyond its possible impact on classrooms. Scientists and many other university-educated professionals see intelligent design as an atavistic attack on modernity itself, and on their place in society. Ian Lance Taylor, a software expert, author, and atheist, says, "Political victories by creationists are scary. . . . When they succeed in legislating the teaching of science through the ballot box, we take a big step toward the establishment of an anti-rational state religion."

Most important, scientists assert that apart from the deleterious effects of intelligent design on classroom teaching, and on the scientific community itself, the theory is, well, bunk.

Numerous highly qualified scientists, often aided by professional associations and publications, offer coherent, evidence-backed explanations of how evolution's "loose ends" can be tied up. For example, scientists argue, organs that appear irreducibly complex—such as the human eye, with its interdependent lens and optical nerve—evolved from simpler light-sensing organs, and gradually discarded superfluous cells and features, just as an arch in a cathedral now stands without the scaffolding that made its construction possible. Similarly, blood coagulation, they say, can be shown to have evolved in steps, as nature mixed and matched proteins and processes already used for other biological purposes.

And scientists note that nothing has seriously challenged the evolution theory—no discovery, for example, of a fossilized cave dweller in the fossilized guts of a T-rex dinosaur; no discovery of a deity's signature in animal viscera.

Moreover, scientists say, intelligent design doesn't even reach the level of a conventional scientific theory, because it fails to describe experiments that would materially prove or disprove its claims. For example, intelligent-design advocates have yet to devise an experiment to show that an intelligent designer does or does not exist. "Whether there is an intelligent designer is not an empirically testable question," Alan Leshner, CEO of the American Association for the Advancement of Science, told *National Journal.*

The Classroom Fight

One of the tactics the scientific community is using to fight off intelligent design is to define science in the law, and especially in state education law, which governs teaching and curricula in the public schools. Scientists want to bar the door to admitting intelligent design as any part of science education. Intelligent-design proponents are "trying to redefine what science is" by allowing supernatural explanations for natural things, Leshner said. "We can't allow that."

Kansas has been one of the primary battlefields in these definitional struggles. In the Sunflower State [of Kansas], where intelligent-design advocates won, then lost, and then won seats on the State Board of Education, science advocates persuaded the board in 2001 to declare, "Science is restricted to explaining only the natural world, using only natural causes . . . because science currently has no tools to test explanations using nonnatural (such as supernatural) causes."

The National Academies, the federally chartered private membership bodies that advise the government on scientific issues, and the National Science Teachers Association [NSTA] are in a battle right now with state officials over the writing of the Kansas Science Education Standards [KSES], which guide the teaching of science in the state's schools. In an October 27 [2005] statement, and in letters to Kansas officials, the academies and the NSTA refused to give copyright permission for officials to use portions of the National Science Education Standards (published by the National Research Council, which is part of the National Academies) or Pathways to Science Standards (published by the NSTA) in the Kansas standards.

Although the latest Kansas standards (which are still [as of 2006] in draft form) are more to the liking of the Academies and the NSTA than the 1999 standards were, the two organizations say the new standards still tilt too much toward intelligent design. [In February 2007, the school board adopted science standards that reflect mainstream scientific views of evolution.]

Leading scientists . . . argue that science should be separated from politics and religion.

"While there is much in the Kansas Science Education Standards that is outstanding and could serve as a model for other states, our primary concern is that the draft KSES inappropriately singles out evolution as a controversial theory despite the strength of the scientific evidence supporting evolution as an explanation for the diversity of life on Earth and its acceptance by an overwhelming majority of scientists," the two organizations wrote in their statement. "The use of the word controversial to suggest that there are flaws in evolution is confusing to students and the public and is entirely misleading. While there may be disagreements among scientists about the exact processes, the theory of evolution has withstood the test of time and new evidence from many scientific disciplines only further supports this robust scientific theory."

Steven Schafersman is president of Texas Citizens for Science, a group that helped to defeat an effort in 2003 to downplay evolution in Texas schoolbooks. Summarizing the efforts of scientists in state capitals around the country, he said, "We want the scientific methods and scientific instruction to be controlled by science."

The Economic Argument

Science groups, such as the American Association for the Advancement of Science and the National Academies, know that the purity of the scientific enterprise is not a big vote-getter. So they're also citing a variety of practical and economic benefits that could be jeopardized by the embrace of intelligent design.

America's high-tech economy, for example, relies on a steady influx of scientifically literate graduates. "The biotech industries need biologically literate customers, workforces, and policy environments, and that's not what they're going to get," if intelligent design gets into the schools, said Glenn Branch, the deputy director of the National Center for Science Education, based in Oakland, Calif. Schafersman, citing Texas as an example, says that the "business community gets behind us [because] they want good science [and] good technology taught in schools [and] reality-based thinking, not faith-based thinking."

It was this economic argument that helped win the day recently [as of January 2006] in the intelligent-design controversy in Dover, Pa. Voters there threw out seven of the eight school board members who had voted to require the teaching of intelligent design in high school. They replaced them with an entirely new slate of candidates who argued that a good science education was necessary to prepare Dover students for success in college and in the workplace.

The Philosophical Argument

Most scientists say that they are not anti-religious and that the vast majority of their colleagues are in the moderate center when it comes to questions of a deity.

The fossil record offers overwhelming evidence for evolution, but no evidence that a God doesn't exist, scientists say. This "middle ground is the one that is embraced by the majority of the scientific community," said Brown University's Miller. Evolution "tells us that we are part of the same process that produced every living thing on Earth; [but] what one makes of that information from a philosophical or theological view depends on a person's philosophical outlook on life."

Leading scientists also argue that science should be separated from politics and religion. "We're the fact people," Leshner said. For example, in debates on the legalization of marijuana and the drug's possible medical benefits for cancer and AIDS patients, "I have no problem telling scientists to stick to facts," Leshner said, because what ought to be done about marijuana "is not a science question." Policy in this instance, he continued, "is made on facts and values."

Intelligent-design advocates see a partial victory in this "stick-to-the-facts" argument cited by scientists. They believe that such a stance is building a wall, albeit a low and weak one perhaps, between the materialist facts of science and its role in politics and policy.

But the pro-evolution side is as much of a Big Tent as the creationism/intelligent-design side is. And the scientists have their diehard activists, too. . . .

In such a big tent, there are bound to be internal disputes and arguments. Some scientists, for example, are informally prodding their more assertive colleagues—such as the outspoken Richard Dawkins, a widely published, U.K.-based proponent of natural evolution—to tone down statements that might cause voters to worry that science is intruding too much into politics and culture, or dictating how controversies should be decided. "It doesn't help that they hear about Richard Dawkins going about saying that people who believe in religion are mistaken or evil," said Michael Ruse, a philosophy professor at Florida State University (Tallahassee) who has written extensively on the history and philosophy of Darwinism. . . .

The political and legal arguments over evolution and intelligent design may be around for a long time, both sides agree, because they are about fundamental questions.

This professional pressure is modest, however, because scientists remain loath to curb other scientists. "Science is like the Catholic Church; it is a very disciplined organization," Ruse said. But, "to a great extent, people would be uncomfortable trying to rein [Dawkins] in."

Still, the informal pressure is having some impact on scientists, Branch said. "I think they're improving, [and] Dawkins has been taking pains" not to offend, he said. "A modicum of caution in not overstating views in dealing with the public is useful."

The Courts

The Supreme Court has enormous power to shape this political fight, and advocates for evolution worry that the Court will step back from its 1968 and 1987 anti-creationism decisions. "All [President George W.] Bush needs to get is one or two votes on his side, and before long, we'll find the justices saying that if people want 'balanced treatment' on intelligent design [in K-12 classrooms], they can have it," Ruse said.

To head this off, "we have to say, 'You can't do [intelligent design in schools], . . . on the grounds that this is a particular form of American Protestant religion,'" Ruse said. The Court should bar schools from teaching that a God exists, he said, just as it should bar scientific claims that God does not exist. . . .

There's no telling how the Supreme Court's decisions may evolve. For example, the Court ruled 5-4 in June [2005] that the display of the Ten Commandments in a courthouse was unconstitutional because any such display must have a secular purpose that is "genuine, not a sham, and not merely secondary to a religious objective." This case, *McCreary County, Kentucky v. American Civil Liberties Union of Kentucky*, seems to raise the bar that the Court set in the 1987 creationism decision in *Edwards v. Aguillard*, which said that curricula must have "a clear secular purpose."

The Court's emphasis on a primary secular purpose ensures that intelligent-design advocates may lose ground whenever they cite religious motivations for their campaign.

But if the high court adopts a hands-off position on intelligent design and lets locals decide what to teach, then the debate at school boards and in state legislatures could expand and intensify.

Scientists and their political allies would lose their judicial trump card and be pitched into a vast number of local political fights, in a nation where creationism is a mainstream notion. Those circumstances "would be much more difficult" than fighting a few courtroom arguments, Schafersman said. "We would have to appeal to common sense."

The political and legal arguments over evolution and intelligent design may be around for a long time, both sides agree, because they are about fundamental questions. The activists on both sides of this dispute, according to Ruse, embody "rival religious responses to a crisis of faith—rival stories of origins, rival judgments about the meaning of human life, rival sets of moral dictates, and above all, . . . rival eschatologies," or theories about humanity's ultimate destiny.

This argument will go on and on because the meaning of life cannot be decided for everyone by a group of scientists, by a black-robed judge, or even by a panel of nine justices. As the Supreme Court itself wrote in its famous 1992 *Planned Parenthood v. Casey* decision on abortion, "At the heart of liberty is the right to define one's own concept of existence, of meaning, of the universe, and of the mystery of human life."

2

The Theory of Intelligent Design Is Based on Science, Not Religion

John G. West

John G. West, formerly a professor of political science, is author of Darwin's Conservatives: The Misguided Quest *and associate director of the Center for Science & Culture at the Discovery Institute, the wellspring for intelligent design advocates.*

Scientific, not religious, principles guide the theory of intelligent design (ID). Supported by a growing number of scientists, ID theory suggests that an intelligent cause better explains some facets of the natural world than the chance processes of natural selection. ID scholars do not want to mandate the teaching of intelligent design. Some states simply want to teach both the strengths and the weakness of the theory of evolution. In fact, ID scholars welcome open debate on the merits of both theories.

There has been a growing public debate about the theory of intelligent design [ID], whether it is science, and whether it should be taught in public schools. President [George W.] Bush's . . . endorsement of teaching about different ideas when studying evolution, including intelligent design, is sure to add fuel to the controversy.

Unfortunately, all the attention has not necessarily led to greater public understanding of the theory of intelligent design or the views of the scientists who support it. Indeed, as

John G. West, "Intelligent Design Is Sorely Misunderstood," *Seattle Post-Intelligencer*, August 9, 2005. Reproduced by permission. http://seattlepi.nwsource.com/opinion/235729_idesign09.html.

intelligent design has become more prominent, foes and friends alike have latched onto it to promote their own agendas. For foes, intelligent design is merely the latest tactic by the "religious right" to use government to impose "creationism" on unsuspecting students and teachers. These critics of intelligent design typically depict scientists who support the theory as zealots determined to twist the findings of science to support their faith in God. If foes are guilty of misappropriating intelligent design, however, so are some of its newfound friends.

Design theory is a scientific inference based on empirical evidence, not religious texts.

As intelligent design has become a household term, a few well-meaning but misguided public officials have conflated the theory of design with creationism or tried to impose it by legislation.

Promoting Serious Misunderstandings

In Utah, a state senator . . . advocated the adoption of what he calls "divine design." In Pennsylvania, the Legislature held hearings on a bill that would allow school districts to mandate the teaching of design. These conflicting voices in the public arena claiming to speak for intelligent design have promoted serious misunderstandings about what the theory actually proposes and what its supporters really want.

The first misunderstanding is that intelligent design is based on religion rather than science. Design theory is a scientific inference based on empirical evidence, not religious texts. The theory proposes that some features of the natural world are best explained as the product of an intelligent cause as opposed to an undirected process such as natural selection. Although controversial, design theory is supported by a growing number of scientists in scientific journals, conference proceedings and books. While intelligent design may have religious implications (just like Darwin's theory), it does not start from religious premises. A second misunderstanding is that proponents of intelligent design theory are crusading to have it required in public schools. In fact, they are doing the opposite.

Discovery Institute, the main research organization supporting ID scholars, opposes efforts to mandate intelligent design. Attempts to mandate teaching about intelligent design only politicize the theory and will hinder fair and open discussion of the merits of the theory among scholars and within the scientific community.

A third misunderstanding is that there are widespread efforts to mandate the teaching of design. In reality, what most states are considering is not teaching design but teaching the weaknesses as well as the strengths of modern Darwinian theory. This is the approach adopted in the science standards of Ohio, Minnesota and New Mexico. It's also the approach under consideration by the Kansas State Board of Education, which [in 2005] heard testimony critical of Darwin's theory from professors of biology, genetics and biochemistry.

While scholars supporting ID are not seeking to impose their views, opponents have tried to silence critics of Darwin's theory using coercion and intimidation. At George Mason University, a biology professor was banned recently [as of 2005] from teaching about intelligent design in her classes. At the Smithsonian Institution, the editor of a biology journal says he faced discrimination and retaliation after accepting for publication a pro-ID article.

Supporters of intelligent design are willing to disavow misguided efforts to impose it by government fiat. Defenders of Darwinism likewise need to reject efforts to enforce their views by trampling on academic freedom. The validity of intelligent design should be decided through fair and open debate, not through legislation enacted by its friends or witch hunts conducted by its foes.

3

Intelligent Design Theory Is Religion, Not Science

New Scientist

New Scientist *is a weekly British science and technology news-magazine.*

The concepts behind the theory of intelligent design (ID) cannot be tested. ID theory does not, therefore, qualify as science. The concept of specified complexity, for example, argues that since it is statistically improbable that complex biological structures emerged through natural selection, they must have been designed. While this notion appears plausible, it cannot be proven and undermines years of often life-saving scientific endeavor. ID is simply disguised creationism. The goal of ID is to promote the idea that God created life, a religious belief, not science.

Now is an uncomfortable time to be a Darwinist in the US. Eighty years after the infamous "monkey trial", when John Scopes was tried for teaching evolution, pressure on Darwin's theory is growing once again. Creationist voices are becoming louder, and a new player is adding to the noise. Intelligent design (ID) uses the language of science to argue that we will never understand nature unless we take the supernatural into account.

Although ID has been around for more than a decade, it has only recently started to make a significant impact on university campuses and school boards, which decide what pupils

New Scientist, "No Contest: It Will Take More than Thinly Disguised Creationism to Defeat Darwin," vol. 187, July 9, 2005, p. 5. Copyright © 2005 Reed Elsevier Business Publishing, Ltd. Reproduced by permission.

are taught. . . . Its advocates argue that various biological structures are too complex to have been created by natural selection and so must have been designed.

The Flaws in ID Theory

To press home their case, they introduce two concepts. "Irreducible complexity" proposes that some molecular systems, such as the one that triggers blood clotting in humans, cannot be broken down into smaller functioning units, and so could not have been created by natural selection. "Specified complexity" uses probability theory to try to show that certain biological structures are so unlikely to have emerged through natural processes that they must have been designed.

These ideas seem plausible on the surface and so can have a powerful impact. Only with scientific understanding does it become clear that they are fundamentally flawed. . . . Crucially, they cannot be tested in any meaningful way, so they cannot qualify as science. If ID ever came to be accepted, it would stifle research. Molecular biologists would call a halt whenever they came across a biological structure that they could not explain and hence must be the work of the "designer". Science as an open-ended pursuit would come to an end, halted by an impenetrable barrier labelled "the designer did it".

ID may qualify as a religious belief, but it is not science.

Advocates of ID have persuaded many people that they have found evolution's Achilles heel. In the name of fairness and balance, they argue, students should be taught the controversy surrounding evolution and ID. This plays to a sense of even-handedness amongst non-scientists. But it is disingenuous. We don't teach children half-baked challenges to other scientific theories that have not run the gauntlet of scientific scrutiny, so why should ID be any different?

The Importance of Evolution

Worse, "teach the controversy" has fostered the notion that there is something fundamentally wrong with Darwin's big idea. Yet this is simply not borne out by the facts. Evolution by natural selection has survived 146 years of scientific scrutiny and has been called the "most important concept in modern biology" by the US National Academies of Sciences.

Evolution has helped us to interpret the fossil record, understand how bacteria become resistant to antibiotics, and described the rapid changes in species taking place before our eyes. . . . It explains some spectacular examples of mal-design, such as cave-dwelling species with functional eyes that are covered by skin flaps. Natural selection has even been harnessed by the biotechnology industry to create new drugs. By contrast, ID has produced not one prediction of value. Evidence against it is mounting from many branches of science, while supporting evidence comes only from a small group of committed ID advocates.

There is no scientific controversy between ID and evolution. The case for teaching them as valid alternatives is no stronger than the case for teaching students about some supposed controversy between astrology and astronomy.

Lurking beneath this debate is the issue of whether religion should make an appearance in science classes—as the creationist movement has long wanted it to. Here it is difficult not to suspect that the people behind ID are being disingenuous in their books and papers. They would rather readers saw ID as purely scientific. Yet one of the governing goals of the Discovery Institute, ID's spiritual home, is to spread the word "that nature and human beings are created by God".

Let's be honest. This is creationism by another name. Tell a class of teenagers that the tail of a bacterium did not evolve but was designed, and who will they think the designer is? ID may qualify as a religious belief, but it is not science. Teach it in philosophy or sociology by all means. Its proper resting place, however, will be in history.

4

The Theory of Intelligent Design Is Neither Religion Nor Science

John Derbyshire

John Derbyshire, a British-born journalist and author, writes for conservative political newsmagazines such as the National Review, *in which Derbyshire describes the intelligent design debate as a conflict "worse than the bloody Middle East."*

The future of intelligent design (ID) either as a scientific theory or a theological principle is limited. ID is simply a critique of evolutionary theory; it submits no testable hypothesis of its own. Indeed, ID scientists are disinclined to submit their theories to peer review. Young scientists will likely reject ID theory because it promises no reproducible results or useful discoveries. Nor does ID offer much as a theology. The God of ID is more like an advanced space alien than the omniscient creator of the universe envisioned by Judaism and Christianity.

This year [2005] contains two notable scientific anniversaries. The one most widely mentioned is the centenary of Albert Einstein's three trailblazing papers in the German scientific journal *Annalen der Physik* on the nature of matter, energy, and motion. Those papers opened up broad new territories for exploration by physicists. The discoveries that followed, and the technology that flowed from those discoveries, helped shape the whole 20th century. Radiation therapy and nuclear weapons, the laser and the personal computer, global positioning satellites and fiber-optic cables—all trace at least part of their lineage to Einstein's papers. The 20th century was the Age of Physics. The first quarter of that century—when dramatic discoveries in the field were coming thick and fast, with theory racing to keep up—was a wonderfully exciting time to be a young physicist.

It seems to me that we are passing from the Age of Physics to the Age of Biology. It is not quite the case that nothing is happening in physics, but certainly there is nothing like the excitement of the early 20th century. Physics seems, in fact, to have got itself into a cul-de-sac, obsessing over theories so mathematically abstruse that nobody even knows how to test them.

The life sciences, by contrast, are blooming, with major new results coming in all the time from genetics, zoology, demography, biochemistry, neuroscience, psychometrics, and other "hot" disciplines. The physics building may be hushed and dark while its inhabitants mentally wrestle with 26-dimensional manifolds, but over at biology the joint is jumpin'. A gifted and ambitious young person of scientific inclination would be well advised to try for a career researching in the life sciences. There is, as one such youngster said to me recently, a lot of low-hanging fruit to be picked. Charles, Murray, in his elegant *New York Times* op-ed piece ..., wrote of the "vibrancy and excitement" of scholarship about innate male-female differences, in contrast to the stale, repetitive nature of research seeking environmental sources for those differences. Sell sociology, buy biology.

The Return of the Evolution Debate

This fizzing vitality in the life sciences is ... very unsettling to the guardians of political correctness. It is at least as disturbing to some Biblical fundamentalists, which brings me to [2005's] second scientific anniversary. The famous "monkey trial" in Dayton, Tenn., happened 80 years ago. . . . John Scopes, a young schoolteacher, was found guilty of violating a state statute forbidding the teaching of evolution theory. Well, well, the wheel turns, and the other day I found myself looking at a newspaper headline that read: "Pa. School Board at the Center of Evolution Debate." The story concerned the town of Dover, Pa., which was sued by the ACLU in federal court at the end of last year over its incorporation of "intelligent design" (I.D.) arguments in the public-school biology curriculum.

It is not surprising that most working scientists turn away from I.D. with a smile and a shrug.

It is odd to be reminded that I.D. is still around. I had written it off as a 1990s fad infecting religious and metaphysical circles, not really touching on science at all, since it framed no hypotheses that could be tested experimentally. The greater part of I.D. is just negative, a critique of the standard model of evolution by natural selection, in which random mutations that add to an organism's chances of survival and reproduction lead to divergences of form and function and eventually to new species. This theory, said I.D. proponents such as Phillip E. Johnson (*Darwin on Trial*, 1991), Michael J. Behe (*Darwin's Black Box*, 1996), and William A. Dembski (*The Design Inference*, 1998), is full of conundrums and unexplained gaps—the mechanisms of mutation, for instance, are poorly understood.

Smile and a Shrug

Biologists are not much impressed with this critique, since conundrums and gaps are normal features of scientific theories. Atomic theory was in considerably worse shape in this regard when Einstein published his three great papers. A few decades of research clarified matters to the point where the theory's practical applicability and predictive value could revolutionize human existence. Nor are scientists much impressed by the facts of Behe's being a biochemist and Dembski's having done postgraduate work in math and physics. (Johnson is a lawyer.) This just recalls Newton's fascination with alchemy and Kepler's work on the Music of the Spheres. Scientists have all sorts of quirky off-duty obsessions.

If the science of I.D. is a joke, the theology is little better.

And I.D. was always off-duty. Scientifically credentialed I.D.-ers have been reluctant to submit their theories to peer review. Kenneth R. Miller, a professor of biology at Brown University and a critic of I.D., wonders why Behe has never presented his ideas to the annual conference of the American Society for Biochemistry and Molecular Biology, as is his right as a member. As Miller explained, "If I thought I had an idea that would completely revolutionize cell biology in the same way that Professor Behe thinks he has an idea that would revolutionize biochemistry, I would be talking about that idea at every single meeting of my peers I could possibly get to." Dembski likewise declines to publicize his research through peer-review conferences and journals. His explanation: "I find I can actually get the turnaround faster by writing a book and getting the ideas expressed there. My books sell well. I get a royalty. And the material gets read more." Ah.

Neither science nor religion ever had much use for I.D. Both will proceed happily on their ways without it.

It is not surprising that most working scientists turn away from I.D. with a smile and a shrug. Phillip Johnson, in a 1992 lecture, predicted that Darwinism would "soon" be thoroughly discredited, leading to a "paradigm shift" and a whole new view of biology. Thirteen years later there is not the faintest trace of a sign that anything like this is going to happen. To the contrary, the fired-up young biologists who will revolutionize our lives in these coming decades take the standard evolutionary model for granted, not only because it is an elegant and parsimonious theory, but because I.D. promises them nothing—no reproducible results, no research leads, no fortune-making discoveries in genomics or neuroscience.

Misplaced Concreteness

If the science of I.D. is a joke, the theology is little better. Its principal characteristic is a flat-footed poverty of imagination. "Don't eff the Ineffable," went the sergeant-major's injunction against blasphemy. With a different reading having nothing to do with blasphemy, effing the Ineffable—what A. N. Whitehead called "misplaced concreteness"—is exactly what the I.D.-ers are up to. Their God is a science-fiction God, a high-I.Q. space alien plodding along a decade or two ahead of our understanding. The God of Judaism and Christianity is infinitely vaster and stranger than that, and far above our poking, groping inquiries into the furniture of our rocky little daytime cosmos. His nature and deeds are as remote from our comprehension as, to quote Darwin himself on this precise point, Newton's laws are from a dog's. The prophet Isaiah held the same opinion: "For my thoughts are not your thoughts, neither are your ways my ways, saith the Lord. For as the heavens are higher than the earth, so are my ways higher than your ways, and my thoughts than your thoughts."

I.D. had its little hour in the spotlight of public curiosity, and will linger on for a while among those who cannot bear the thought that living tissue might be a part of the natural universe, under natural laws. Neither science nor religion ever had much use for I.D. Both will proceed happily on their ways without it.

5

Evolution Is an Accepted Fact

Richard Dawkins

Richard Dawkins, a British evolutionary biologist, science writer, outspoken atheist, secular humanist, and skeptic, has written numerous books that support evolution, including The Blind Watchmaker *and* Climbing Mount Improbable.

Evolution is no longer a theory to be proven but an agreed-upon fact. That evolutionary theory is an improbable explanation for nature's complexity does not alter the fact that fossil records support the theory's claims. There is no evidence whatsoever to support intelligent design—an equally improbable explanation of life's complexity. While for some people evolution may be unpalatable and for others a potentially dangerous weapon if used as a political or moral doctrine, it remains, among real scientists, an accepted fact.

The world is divided into things that look as though somebody designed them (wings and wagon-wheels, hearts and televisions), and things that just happened through the unintended workings of physics (mountains and rivers, sand dunes, and solar systems). Mount Rushmore belonged firmly in the second category until the sculptor Gutzon Borglum carved it into the first. Charles Darwin moved in the other direction. He discovered a way in which the unaided laws of physics—the laws according to which things "just happen"—could, in the fullness of geologic time, come to mimic deliberate design. The illusion of design is so successful that to this day most

Richard Dawkins, "The Illusions of Design," *Natural History,* vol. 114, November, 2005, pp. 35–7. Copyright the American Museum of Natural History 2005. Reproduced by permission.

Americans (including, significantly, many influential and rich Americans) stubbornly refuse to believe it *is* an illusion. To such people, if a heart (or an eye or a bacterial flagellum) looks designed, that's proof enough that it is designed.

The Simplicity of Darwin's Theory

No wonder Thomas Henry Huxley, "Darwin's bulldog," was moved to chide himself on reading the *Origin of Species*: "How extremely stupid not to have thought of that." And Huxley was the least stupid of men. The breathtaking power and reach of Darwin's idea—extensively documented in the field, as Jonathan Weiner reports in *Evolution in Action* . . .—is matched by its audacious simplicity. You can write it out in a phrase: nonrandom survival of randomly varying hereditary instructions for building embryos. Yet, given the opportunities afforded by deep time, this simple little algorithm generates prodigies of complexity, elegance, and diversity of apparent design. True design, the kind we see in a knapped flint, a jet plane, or a personal computer, turns out to be a manifestation of an entity—the human brain—that itself was never designed, but is an evolved product of Darwin's mill.

Paradoxically, the extreme simplicity of what the philosopher Daniel C. Dennett called Darwin's dangerous idea may be its greatest barrier to acceptance. People have a hard time believing that so simple a mechanism could deliver such powerful results.

The arguments of creationists, including those creationists who cloak their pretensions under the politically devious phrase "intelligent-design theory," repeatedly return to the same big fallacy. Such-and-such looks designed. Therefore it was designed. To pursue my paradox, there is a sense in which the skepticism that often greets Darwin's idea is a measure of its greatness.

Paraphrasing the twentieth-century population geneticist Ronald A. Fisher, natural selection is a mechanism for generating improbability on an enormous scale. *Improbable* is pretty much a synonym for *unbelievable*. Any theory that explains the highly improbable is asking to be disbelieved by those who don't understand it.

Explaining the Improbable

Yet the highly improbable does exist in the real world, and it must be explained. Adaptive improbability—complexity—is precisely the problem that any theory of life must solve and that natural selection, uniquely as far as science knows, does solve. In truth, it is intelligent design that is the biggest victim of the argument from improbability. Any entity capable of deliberately designing a living creature, to say nothing of a universe, would have to be hugely complex in its own right.

If, as the maverick astronomer Fred Hoyle mistakenly thought, the spontaneous origin of life is as improbable as a hurricane blowing through a junkyard and having the luck to assemble a Boeing 747, then a divine designer is the ultimate Boeing 747. The designer's spontaneous origin *ex nihilo* would have to be even more improbable than the most complex of his alleged creations. Unless, of course, he relied on natural selection to do his work for him! And in that case, one might pardonably wonder (though this is not the place to pursue the question), does he need to exist at all?

The achievement of nonrandom natural selection is to tame chance. By smearing out the luck, breaking down the improbability into a large number of small steps—each one somewhat improbable but not ridiculously so—natural selection ratchets up the improbability.

As the generations unfold, ratcheting takes the cumulative improbability up to levels that—in the absence of the ratcheting—would exceed all sensible credence.

Many people don't understand such nonrandom cumulative ratcheting. They think natural selection is a theory of chance, so no wonder they don't believe it! The battle that we biologists face, in our struggle to convince the public and their elected representatives that evolution is a fact, amounts to the battle to convey to them the power of Darwin's ratchet—the blind watchmaker—to propel lineages up the gentle slopes of Mount Improbable.

Gaps in Understanding

The misapplied argument from improbability is not the only one deployed by creationists. They are quite fond of gaps, both literal gaps in the fossil record and gaps in their understanding of what Darwinism is all about. In both cases the (lack of) logic in the argument is the same. They allege a gap or deficiency in the Darwinian account. Then, without even inquiring whether intelligent design suffers from the same deficiency, they award victory to the rival "theory" by default. Such reasoning is no way to do science. But science is precisely not what creation "scientists," despite the ambitions of their intelligent-design bullyboys, are doing.

> [Some] evolutionists have opposed Darwinism as a political and moral doctrine just as passionately as they have advocated its scientific truth.

In the case of fossils, as Donald R. Prothero documents in "The Fossils Say Yes," . . . today's biologists are more fortunate than Darwin was in having access to beautiful series of transitional stages: almost cinematic records of evolutionary changes in action. Not all transitions are so attested, of course—hence the vaunted gaps. Some small animals just don't fossilize, their phyla are known only from modern specimens: their history is one big gap. The equivalent gaps for any creationist or intelligent-design theory would be the absence of a cinematic record of God's every move on the morning that he created, for example, the bacterial flagellar motor. Not only is there no such divine videotape: there is a complete absence of evidence of any kind for intelligent design.

Absence of evidence *for* is not positive evidence *against*, of course. Positive evidence against evolution could easily be found—if it exists. Fisher's contemporary and rival J.B.S. Haldane was asked by a Popperian zealot [A Popperian is one who subscribes to the philosophy of Sir Karl Raimund Popper, who believed that scientific theory is irreducibly conjectural or hypothetical. Logically, no number of positive outcomes at the level of experimental testing can confirm a scientific theory, but a single counterexample is logically decisive: it shows the theory, from which the implication is derived, to be false.] what would falsify evolution. Haldane quipped, "Fossil rabbits in the Precambrian." No such fossil has ever been found, of course, despite numerous searches for anachronistic species.

Barriers to Accepting the Truth

There are other barriers to accepting the truth of Darwinism. Many people cannot bear to think that they are cousins not just of chimpanzees and monkeys, but of tapeworms, spiders, and bacteria. The unpalatability of a proposition, however, has no bearing on its truth. I personally find the idea of cousinship to all living species positively agreeable, but neither my warmth toward it, nor the cringing of a creationist, has the slightest bearing on its truth.

One thing all scientists agree upon is the fact of evolution itself.

The same could be said of political or moral objections to Darwinism. "Tell children they are nothing more than animals and they will behave like animals." I do not for a moment accept that the conclusion follows from the premise. But even if it did, once again, a disagreeable consequence cannot undermine the truth of a premise. Some have said that Hitler founded his political philosophy on Darwinism. This is nonsense: doctrines of racial superiority in no way follow from natural selection, properly understood. Nevertheless, a good case can be made that a society run on Darwinian lines would be a very disagreeable society in which to live. But, yet again, the unpleasantness of a proposition has no bearing on its truth.

Huxley, George C. Williams, and other evolutionists have opposed Darwinism as a political and moral doctrine just as passionately as they have advocated its scientific truth. I count myself in that company. Science needs to understand natural selection as a force in nature, the better to oppose it as a normative force in politics. Darwin himself expressed dismay at the callousness of natural selection: "What a book a Devil's Chaplain might write on the clumsy, wasteful, blundering low & horridly cruel works of nature!"

Darwin's Achievements

In spite of the success and admiration that he earned, and despite his large and loving family, Darwin's life was not an especially happy one. Troubled about genetic deterioration in general and the possible effects of inbreeding closer to home, . . . and tormented by illness and bereavement, . . . Darwin's achievements seem all the more. He even found the time to excel as an experimenter, particularly with plants. . . . Even without his major theoretical achievements, Darwin would have won lasting recognition as an experimenter, albeit an experimenter with the style of a gentlemanly amateur, which might not find favor with modern journal referees.

As for his major theoretical achievements, of course, the details of our understanding have moved on since Darwin's time. That was particularly the case during the synthesis of Darwinism with Mendelian digital genetics. And beyond the synthesis . . . Darwinism proves to be a flourishing population of theories, itself undergoing rapid evolutionary change.

In any developing science there are disagreements. But scientists—and here is what separates real scientists from the pseudoscientists of the school of intelligent design—always know what evidence it would take to change their minds. One thing all real scientists agree upon is the fact of evolution itself. It is a fact that we are cousins of gorillas, kangaroos, starfish, and bacteria. Evolution is as much a fact as the heat of the Sun. It is not a theory, and for pity's sake, let's stop confusing the philosophically naive by calling it so. Evolution is a fact.

6

Evolution Is a Flawed Theory

William A. Dembski

William A. Dembski, a professor of science and theology at Southern Seminary in Louisville, Kentucky, is editor of Uncommon Dissent: Intellectuals Who Find Darwinism Unconvincing *and co-editor with Michael Ruse of* Debating Design: From Darwin to DNA. *At Baylor University, Dembski headed the first intelligent design think-tank.*

Like alchemists, who hoped to transform lead into gold, evolutionists have failed to identify with sufficient specificity the process by which one organism evolves into another. To believe without proof that life emerged from material causes rather than a designing intelligence is not science, but metaphysics. Without specifying a cause, evolutionists cannot empirically prove that one life emerged from another or that nonliving chemicals combined to form the first life form. As long as evolution resorts to an unspecified mechanism to explain the origin and evolution of life, it will resemble alchemy more than science.

In its heyday alchemy was a comprehensive theory of transmutation describing not only transformations of base into precious metals but also transformations of the soul up and down the great chain of being. Alchemy was not just a physics but also a metaphysics. . . .

Alchemy's metaphysical pretensions aside, to include alchemy as part of the natural sciences is nowadays regarded as

William A. Dembski, "Evolution as Alchemy," *designinference.com*, June 23, 2006. Reproduced by permission. www.designinference.com/documents/2006.06.Evolution_as_Alchemy.pdf.

hopelessly misguided. The scientific community rejects alchemy as superstition and commends itself for having successfully debunked it. For scientists the problem with alchemy is that it fails to specify the processes by which transmutations are supposed to take place. . . .

Alchemy by Another Name

Officially, the scientific community rejects alchemy and has rejected it since the rise of modern science. Unofficially, however, the scientific community has had a much harder time eradicating it. Indeed, I will argue that alchemical thinking pervades the fields of chemical and biological evolution. This is not to deny that biological systems evolve. But unless the process by which one organism evolves into another (or by which nonliving chemicals organize into a first living form) is specified, evolution remains an empty word. And given that such specificity is often lacking, much (though not all) of what currently falls under evolutionary theory is alchemy by another name.

Alchemy followed a certain logic, and it is important to see the fallacy inherent in that logic. The problem with alchemy was not its failure to understand the causal process responsible for a transformation. . . .

Things transform into other things. Sometimes we can explain the process by which the transformation takes place. At other times we cannot. Sometimes the process requires an intelligent agent, sometimes no intelligent agent is required. Thus, a process that arranges randomly strewn Scrabble pieces into meaningful English sentences requires a guiding intelligence. On the other hand, the process by which water crystallizes into ice requires no guiding intelligence—lowering the temperature sufficiently is all that is needed. It is not alchemy that transforms water into ice. Nor is it alchemy that transforms randomly strewn Scrabble pieces into meaningful sentences. . . .

The Problem with Alchemy

What, then, is the problem with alchemy? Alchemy's problem is its lack of causal specificity. Causal specificity means specifying a cause sufficient to account for an effect in question. Often we can specify the cause of an effect even if we cannot explain how the cause produces the effect. . . .

Alchemy eschews causal specificity. Consider the standard example of alchemical transformation, the transmutation of lead into gold. There is no logical impossibility that prevents potions and furnaces from acting on lead and turning it into gold. It may just be that we have overlooked some property of lead that, in combination with the right ingredients, allows it to be transformed into gold. But the alchemists of old never specified the precise causal antecedents that would bring about this transformation. Consequently, they lacked any compelling evidence that the transformation was even possible. . . .

Causal specificity was evident in the examples considered earlier: Water cooled below zero degrees Celsius is sufficient to account for it turning to ice. A random collection of Scrabble pieces left in the hands of a literate, nonhandicapped English speaker is sufficient to account for the Scrabble pieces spelling a coherent English sentence. . . . In each of these cases the causal antecedent is specified and accounts for the effect in question. We may not be able to explain how the cause that was specified produces its effect, but we know that it does so nonetheless.

The Alchemist's Conviction

But how do we get from causal antecedents like lead, potions, and furnaces and end up with gold? The alchemists' conviction was that if one could find just the right ingredients to combine with lead, lead would transform into gold. Thereafter the transformation could be performed at will and the alchemist who discovered the secret of transmutation would be rich (until, that is, the secret got out and gold became so common that it too became a base metal). Discovering the secret of transmutation was the alchemist's deepest hope. The interesting question for this essay, however, is the alchemist's reason for that hope. Why were alchemists so confident that the transmutation from base into precious metals could even be effected? From our vantage, we judge their enterprise a failure and one that had no possibility of success (contemporary solid state physics giving the coup de grace). But why were they unshaken in their conviction that with the few paltry means at their disposal (particle accelerators not being among them), they could transform base into precious metals? Put another way, why, lacking causal specificity, did they think the transformation could be effected at all?

Alchemy continues to flourish to this day in the fields of chemical and biological evolution.

Without causal specificity, one has no empirical justification for affirming that a transformation can be effected. At the same time, without causal specificity, one has no empirical justification for denying that a transformation can be effected. There is no way to demonstrate with complete certainty that Dr. Jekyll cannot transform into Mr. Hyde by some unspecified process. Lack of causal specificity leaves one without the means to judge whether a desired transformation can or cannot be effected. Any conviction about the desired transformation being possible, much less inevitable, must therefore derive from considerations other than a causal analysis. But from where?

Enter metaphysics. It is no secret that the motivation behind alchemy was never scientific (as we use the term nowadays) but metaphysical. Alchemy is a corollary of Neoplatonic metaphysics. Neoplatonism held to a great chain of being in which all reality emanates from God (conceived of as the One) and ultimately returns to God. The great chain of being is strictly hierarchical, so that for any two distinct items in the chain one is higher than the other. Now consider lead and gold. Gold is higher on the chain than lead (lead is a base metal, gold is a precious metal). Moreover, since everything is returning to God, lead is returning to God and on its way to God will pass through gold. Consequently, there is a natural pull for lead to get to gold on its way to God. The alchemist's task is therefore not to violate nature, but simply to help nature along. All lead needs is a small suitable catalyst to achieve gold. The modest means by which alchemists hoped to achieve the transformation of lead into gold thus seemed entirely reasonable (in particular, no particle accelerators would be required).

A Logical Fallacy

Here, then, is the fallacy in alchemy's logic. Alchemy relinquishes causal specificity, yet confidently asserts that an unspecified process will yield a desired transformation. Lacking causal specificity, the alchemist has no empirical grounds for holding that the desired transformation can be effected. Even so, the alchemist remains convinced that the transformation can be effected because prior metaphysical beliefs ensure that some process, though for now unspecified, must effect the desired transformation. In short, metaphysics guarantees the transformation even if the empirical evidence is against it.

Origin-of-life researchers have yet to specify the chemical pathways that supposedly originated life.

Alchemy continues to flourish to this day in the fields of chemical and biological evolution. Whereas classical alchemy was concerned with transforming base into precious metals, evolution is concerned with transforming batches of chemicals into organisms and then organisms into other organisms. Now, I do not want to give the impression that evolution is a completely disreputable concept. The concept has applications that are entirely innocent. Consider, for instance, finches evolving stronger beaks to break harder nuts or insects developing insecticide resistance. Evolution in such cases is nonproblematic. Why? Because of causal specificity. Microevolutionary changes like this happen repeatedly and reliably. Given certain organisms placed in certain environments with certain selective pressures, certain predictable changes will result. We may not understand the precise biochemical factors that make such microevolutionary changes possible. But the causal antecedents that produce microevolutionary changes are clearly specified. So long as we have causal specificity, evolution is a perfectly legitimate concept.

A Lack of Causal Specificity

But what about evolution without causal specificity? Consider, for instance, chemical evolution as an explanation for the origin of life. For much of the scientific community, the presumption is that life organized itself via undirected chemical pathways and thus apart from any designing intelligence. Yet, unlike the causal specificity that obtains for microevolutionary processes, origin-of-life researchers have yet to specify the chemical pathways that supposedly originated life. Despite a vast literature on the origin of life, causally specific proposals for just what those chemical pathways might be are sorely absent. Which is not to say that there have not been any proposals. In fact, there are too many of them. RNA worlds, clay templates, hydrothermal vents, and numerous other materialistic scenarios have all been proposed to account for the chemical evolution of life. Yet, none of these scenarios is detailed enough to be seriously criticized or tested. In short, they all lack causal specificity.

In the absence of causal specificity, the logic of evolution parallels the logic of alchemy. Evolution, like alchemical transformation, is a relational notion. Alchemy never said that gold just magically materializes. Rather, it said that there are antecedents (lead, potions, furnaces) from which it materializes. So too evolution does not say that organisms just magically materialize. Rather, it says that there are antecedents (in the case of the origin of life, it posits RNA worlds, clay templates, hydrothermal vents, etc.) from which life materializes. Thus, to say that something evolves is to say what it evolves from: just as for the alchemist gold "evolves" (again, in its literal etymological sense) from lead plus some other (unspecified) things, so for the contemporary origin-of-life researcher organisms "evolve" from suitable (albeit unspecified) batches of prebiotic chemicals.

"X evolves" is therefore an incomplete sentence. It needs to be completed by reading "X evolves from Y." Moreover, the claim that X evolves from Y remains vacuous until one specifies Y and can demonstrate that Y is sufficient to account for X. Lowering the temperature of water below zero degrees Celsius is causally specific and adequately accounts for the freezing of water. On the other hand, a complete set of the building materials for a house does not suffice to account for a house—additionally what is needed is an architectural plan (drawn up by an architect) as well as assembly instructions (executed by a contractor) to implement the plan. Likewise, with the origin of life, it does no good simply to have the building blocks for life (e.g., nucleotide bases or amino acids). The means for organizing those building blocks into a coherent system (i.e., a living organism) need to be specified as well.

Evolution's Metaphysics

Given the pervasive lack of causal specificity in origin-of-life studies, why are so many origin-of-life researchers supremely confident that material causes are even up to the task of originating life?... The singular lack of success of science in elucidating the origin-of-life problem makes this overweening confidence all the more puzzling if we try to understand it [in] light of the skepticism and tentativeness with which the scientific method tells us to approach hypotheses.

Science needs to be a free inquiry into all the possibilities that might operate in nature.

On the other hand, if, as I am suggesting, there is a precise parallel between evolution and alchemy, then this confidence is perfectly understandable, because in that case it flows from a prior metaphysical commitment that is both inviolable and nonnegotiable. What prior metaphysical commitment ensures that material causes, though for now unspecified, must effect the desired evolutionary transformations? In the case of alchemy, the prior metaphysical commitment was Neoplatonism. In the case of chemical and biological evolution, the prior metaphysical commitment is, obviously, materialism. Materialism is the view that material causes at base govern the world. Given materialism as a prior metaphysical commitment, it follows that life must evolve through purely material causes. But that commitment, like the alchemists' commitment to Neoplatonism, is highly problematic. . . .

Restricting the Range of Solutions

Because the origin of life is an open problem, the reference to "purely material causes" lacks, to be sure, causal specificity. But there is a deeper problem, and that is the imposition of an arbitrary restriction. The problem with claiming that life has emerged from purely material causes is not that it admits ignorance about an unsolved problem, but that *it artificially restricts the range of possible solutions to that problem*; namely, it requires that solutions limit themselves to purely material causes. This is an arbitrary and metaphysically driven restriction. Life has emerged via purely material causes. How do we know that? In general, to hypothesize that X results from Y remains pure speculation until the process that brings about X from Y is causally specified. Until then, to impose restrictions on the types of causal factors that may or may not be employed in Y to bring about X is arbitrary and certain to frustrate scientific inquiry.

In this respect evolution is even more culpable than alchemy. Alchemy sought to transform lead into gold, but left open the means by which the transformation could be effected (though in practice alchemists hoped the transformation could be effected through the modest technical means at their disposal). Evolution, on the other hand, seeks to transform nonlife into life and then organisms into very different organisms, but—when biased by materialism—excludes any place for intelligence or teleology in the transformation. Such a restriction is gratuitous given evolution's lack of causal specificity in accounting not only for the origin of life but also for the macroevolutionary changes supposedly responsible for life's subsequent diversification.

Perhaps materialism will eventually be vindicated and the great open problems of evolution will submit to purely materialistic solutions. But in the absence of causal specificity, there is no reason to let materialism place such restrictions on scientific theorizing. It is restrictions like these—typically unspoken, metaphysically motivated, and at odds with free scientific inquiry—that need to be resisted and exposed. Science must not degenerate into applied materialistic philosophy, which is exactly what it does at the hands of today's alchemists—the materialistic evolutionists who hold their views not on the basis of empirical evidence but because of a prior metaphysical commitment to materialism. Science needs to be a free inquiry into all the possibilities that might operate in nature. Design, therefore, needs to be kept as a live possibility in scientific discussions of biological origins.

The origin of life is just one instance of evolution without causal specificity. The evolution of human consciousness and language from the neurophysiology of primate ancestors is another. The most widely debated instance is the evolution of increasingly complex life forms from simpler ones. Although the Darwinian mutation-selection mechanism is supposed to handle such cases of evolution, it encounters the same failure of causal specificity endemic to alchemy. . . . The lesson of alchemy should be plain: Causal specificity cannot be redeemed in the coin of metaphysics, be it Neoplatonic or materialistic.

7

The Theory of Evolution
Is Ideology, Not Science

Christoph Schönborn

Christoph Schönborn, an influential Austrian Roman Catholic cardinal, participated in the 2005 papal conclave that selected Pope Benedict XVI. Schönborn's New York Times *editorial excerpted below created considerable controversy among Catholics.*

Any theory that explains the evolution of life as an unguided process left to chance is not science, but ideology. Scientific observation of the evolution of living things reveals a direction and purpose that suppose a creator. Indeed, human reason drives us to discover our origins and God's existence and His divine purpose. To leave human origins to chance and random variation is to give up on the search to understand the world around us. Such a belief is not science, but the abdication of human intelligence.

Ever since 1996, when Pope John Paul II said that evolution (a term he did not define) was "more than just a hypothesis," defenders of neo-Darwinian dogma have often invoked the supposed acceptance—or at least acquiescence—of the Roman Catholic Church when they defend their theory as somehow compatible with Christian faith.

But this is not true. The Catholic Church, while leaving to science many details about the history of life on earth, proclaims that by the light of reason the human intellect can readily and clearly discern purpose and design in the natural world, including the world of living things.

Evolution in the sense of common ancestry might be true, but evolution in the neo-Darwinian sense—an unguided, unplanned process of random variation and natural selection—is not. Any system of thought that denies or seeks to explain away the overwhelming evidence for design in biology is ideology, not science.

The Teachings of Pope John Paul II

Consider the real teaching of our beloved John Paul. While his rather vague and unimportant 1996 letter about evolution is always and everywhere cited, we see no one discussing these comments from a 1985 general audience that represents his robust teaching on nature:

"All the observations concerning the development of life lead to a similar conclusion. The evolution of living beings, of which science seeks to determine the stages and to discern the mechanism, presents an internal finality which arouses admiration. This finality which directs beings in a direction for which they are not responsible or in charge, obliges one to suppose a Mind which is its inventor, its creator."

He went on: "To all these indications of the existence of God the Creator, some oppose the power of chance or of the proper mechanisms of matter. To speak of chance for a universe which presents such a complex organization in its elements and such marvelous finality in its life would be equivalent to giving up the search for an explanation of the world as it appears to us. In fact, this would be equivalent to admitting effects without a cause. It would be to abdicate human intelligence, which would thus refuse to think and to seek a solution for its problems."

Note that in this quotation the word "finality" is a philosophical term synonymous with final cause, purpose or design. In comments at another general audience a year later,

John Paul concludes, "It is clear that the truth of faith about creation is radically opposed to the theories of materialistic philosophy. These view the cosmos as the result of an evolution of matter reducible to pure chance and necessity."

Finding Design in Nature

Naturally, the authoritative Catechism of the Catholic Church agrees: "Human intelligence is surely already capable of finding a response to the question of origins. The existence of God the Creator can be known with certainty through his works, by the light of human reason." It adds: "We believe that God created the world according to his wisdom. It is not the product of any necessity whatever, nor of blind fate or chance."

In an unfortunate new twist on this old controversy, neo-Darwinists recently [as of 2005] have sought to portray our new pope, Benedict XVI, as a satisfied evolutionist. They have quoted a sentence about common ancestry from a 2004 document of the International Theological Commission, pointed out that Benedict was at the time head of the commission, and concluded that the Catholic Church has no problem with the notion of "evolution" as used by mainstream biologists—that is, synonymous with neo-Darwinism.

Scientific theories that try to explain away the appearance of design as the result of "chance and necessity" are not scientific at all.

The commission's document, however, reaffirms the perennial teaching of the Catholic Church about the reality of design in nature. Commenting on the widespread abuse of John Paul's 1996 letter on evolution, the commission cautions that "the letter cannot be read as a blanket approbation of all theories of evolution, including those of a neo-Darwinian provenance which explicitly deny to divine providence any truly causal role in the development of life in the universe."

Furthermore, according to the commission, "An unguided evolutionary process—one that falls outside the bounds of divine providence—simply cannot exist."

Indeed, in the homily at his installation just a few weeks ago [April 24, 2005], Benedict proclaimed: "We are not some casual and meaningless product of evolution. Each of us is the result of a thought of God. Each of us is willed, each of us is loved, each of us is necessary."

Throughout history the church has defended the truths of faith given by Jesus Christ. But in the modern era, the Catholic Church is in the odd position of standing in firm defense of reason as well. In the 19th century, the First Vatican Council taught a world newly enthralled by the "death of God" that by the use of reason alone mankind could come to know the reality of the Uncaused Cause, the First Mover, the God of the philosophers.

Now at the beginning of the 21st century, faced with scientific claims like neo-Darwinism and the multiverse hypothesis in cosmology invented to avoid the overwhelming evidence for purpose and design found in modern science, the Catholic Church will again defend human reason by proclaiming that the immanent design evident in nature is real. Scientific theories that try to explain away the appearance of design as the result of "chance and necessity" are not scientific at all, but, as John Paul put it, an abdication of human intelligence.

8

Critical Analysis of Evolutionary Theory Should Be Taught in Public Schools

Jonathan Witt

Jonathan Witt, a fellow at the Discovery Institute, the fountain-head for intelligent-design supporters, is coauthor of A Meaningful World: How the Arts and Sciences Reveal the Genius of Nature.

The critical analysis of ideas is crucial to a good education. Schools should therefore expose students to arguments both for and against evolutionary theory. For example, students should know that biologists have not been able to describe, in detail, the continuous evolutionary path to complex life forms such as mammals. If overwhelming evidence indeed supports the theory of evolution, Darwinists should not be afraid to expose students to the theory's unsolved questions.

As a doctoral student at the University of Kansas in the '90s, I found that my professors came in all stripes, and that lazy ideas didn't get off easy. If some professor wanted to preach the virtues of communism after it had failed miserably in the Soviet Union, he was free to do so, but students were also free to hear from other professors who critically analyzed that position.

Conversely, students who believed capitalism and democracy were the great engines of human progress had to grapple

Jonathan Witt, "What Are Darwinists So Afraid Of?" *WorldNetDaily*, July 27, 2006. Reproduced by permission. www.worldnetdaily.com/news/article.asp?ARTICLE_ID=5124.4

with the best arguments against that view, meaning that in the end, they were better able to defend their beliefs.

A Marketplace of Ideas

Such a free marketplace of ideas is crucial to a solid education, and it's what the current Kansas science standards promote. These standards, like those adopted in other states and supported by a three-to-one margin among U.S. voters, don't call for teaching intelligent design. They call for schools to equip students to critically analyze modern evolutionary theory by teaching the evidence both for and against it.

The standards are good for students and good for science.

Some want to protect Darwinism from the competitive marketplace by overturning the critical-analysis standards. My hope is that these efforts will merely lead students to ask, What's the evidence they don't want us to see?

Exposing Gaps in Evolution Theory

Under the new standards, they'll get an answer. For starters, many high-school biology textbooks have presented Haeckel's 19th century embryo drawings, the four-winged fruit fly, peppered moths hidden on tree trunks and the evolving beak of the Galapagos finch as knockdown evidence for Darwinian evolution. What they don't tell students is that these icons of evolution have been discredited, not by Christian fundamentalists but by mainstream evolutionists.

We now know that 1) Haeckel faked his embryo drawings; 2) Anatomically mutant fruit flies are always dysfunctional; 3) Peppered moths don't rest on tree trunks (the photographs were staged); and 4) the finch beaks returned to normal after the rains returned—no net evolution occurred. Like many species, the average size fluctuates within a given range.

This is microevolution, the age-old observation of change within species. Macroevolution refers to the evolution of fundamentally new body plans and anatomical parts. Biology textbooks use instances of microevolution such as the Galapagos finches to paper over the fact that biologists have never observed, or even described in theoretical terms, a detailed, continually functional pathway to fundamentally new forms like mammals, wings and bats. This is significant because modern Darwinism claims that all life evolved from a common ancestor by a series of tiny, useful genetic mutations.

Textbooks also trumpet a few "missing links" discovered between groups. What they don't mention is that Darwin's theory requires untold millions of missing links, evolving one tiny step at a time. Yes, the fossil record is incomplete, but even mainstream evolutionists have asked, why is it selectively incomplete in just those places where the need for evidence is most crucial?

Opponents of the new science standards don't want Kansas high-school students grappling with that question. They argue that such problems aren't worth bothering with because Darwinism is supported by "overwhelming evidence." But if the evidence is overwhelming, why shield the theory from informed critical analysis? Why the campaign to mischaracterize the current standards and replace them with a plan to spoonfeed students Darwinian pabulum strained of uncooperative evidence?

The truly confident Darwinist should be eager to tell students, "Hey, notice these crucial unsolved problems in modern evolutionary theory. Maybe one day you'll be one of the scientists who discovers a solution."

Confidence is as confidence does.

9

Intelligent Design Should Not Be Taught in Public School Science Classrooms

Alan J. Leshner

Alan J. Leshner, former director of the National Institute on Drug Abuse, is chief executive officer of the American Association for the Advancement of Science and executive publisher of Science *magazine.*

Science classrooms are for the teaching of science. Inserting a belief system such as intelligent design into the science classroom conflicts with the principles of science education. In science classes, students learn that scientists do not accept a theory based on what they want to believe, but only after repeated observation and experiments provide evidence to support the theory. Since intelligent design theory has yet to offer any testable hypotheses, it remains a matter of belief, not science, and as such should not be taught in science classes.

Science classrooms are for the teaching of science, and intelligent design is not science-based. Science involves well-developed methods of inquiry for explaining the natural world in a systematic, testable fashion. The theory of evolution is based on such rigorous sifting of evidence.

But advocates of intelligent design, while seeking to cloak themselves in the language of science, have yet to propose testable hypotheses that can be subjected to the methods of experimental science. Intelligent design presupposes that an intelligent, supernatural agent is responsible for biological structures and processes deemed to be "irreducibly complex." But whether such an intelligent designer exists is a matter of belief or faith, not science.

A Place for Science and Religion

In science classrooms, students learn that scientists reject or accept theories according to how well they explain the evidence rather than on what the researchers would like to believe. Students learn that a scientific theory, such as evolution or gravity, is much more than just an educated guess. A theory is accepted only after repeated observation and experiment.

Discussion of intelligent design may be appropriate in a class devoted to history, philosophy or social studies but not in a biology class. Science teachers should not be asked to teach religious ideas or to balance the scientific theory of evolution against an untestable alternative.

Many scientists are deeply religious and see scientific investigation and religious faith as complementary components of a well-rounded life. There is a place for discussing the role of science and religion in American life, but the science classroom should remain a place for teachers to nurture the spirit of curiosity and inquiry that has marked American science since the days of Benjamin Franklin and Thomas Jefferson.

Our children deserve a first-class science education. Efforts to redefine science by inserting a particular belief into the biology curriculum are in direct conflict with science standards recommended by both the National Academy of Sciences and the [American Association for the Advancement of Science] AAAS.

Proponents of intelligent design are doing more than attack evolution. They also are undermining essential methods of science by challenging its reliance on observable causes to explain the world around us.

America's students must be taught to distinguish between true science and a system of belief based on faith. At a time when the United States faces increasing global competition in science and technology, public school science classrooms should remain free of ideological interference and dedicated to the rigor that has made American science the envy of the world.

10

Intelligent Design Should Be Taught in Religion Classes, Not Science

Michael Ruse

Michael Ruse, professor of philosophy and zoology at Florida State University and editor of the journal Biology & Philosophy, *is author of many books, including* Monad to Man: The Concept of Progress in Evolutionary Biology *and* Taking Darwin Seriously: The Evolution-Creation Struggle.

Intelligent design (ID) theory asserts that the intervention of an intelligent designer is necessary to explain the complexity of life on earth. The writing of ID advocates has made clear that the designer they envision is the Christian God. Thus, while schools might teach intelligent design in religion classes, they should not teach ID in science classes. Indeed, the goal of ID is not to advance science, but to advocate beliefs that some people value. Thus, teaching ID in anything other than a course on religion is unconstitutional.

So-called intelligent design [ID] is getting a lot of media attention in America at the moment. Its supporters are pushing hard to have it introduced into the science classes of the nation's public schools, there to be taught alongside evolutionary theory. ID supporters argue that students should be "taught the issues"—meaning they should be exposed to the various beliefs that Americans have about biological origins—and then allowed to decide for themselves.

Michael Ruse, "Keep Intelligent Design Out of Science Classes," *beliefnet.com*, 2006. This article appeared originally on www.beliefnet.com, the leading website for faith, spirituality, inspiration & more. Used with permisson. All rights reserved. www.beliefnet.com/story/172/story_17244_1.html.

The ID movement is having considerable success in its aims. Several school boards in states as different as Kansas and Pennsylvania have decided (or are in the process of deciding [as of 2006]) that ID should be taught in biology classes. [On December 20, 2005, federal judge John E. Jones ruled that it was unconstitutional for a Pennsylvania school district to present intelligent design as an alternative to evolution in high school biology courses because it is a religious viewpoint that advances "a particular version of Christianity." In 2005, Kansas adopted science standards that painted evolution as a flawed theory. In February 2007, the school board adopted science standards that reflect mainstream scientific views of evolution.] . . . The movement has gained significant support, for President George W. Bush has agreed publicly that ID should be taught. . . .

The ID Movement

Two questions should be asked. What is intelligent design? Should it be taught in schools? Answering the first, the claim is that in the history of life on this planet, at some point or points, an intelligence intervened to move things along. This was necessary, argue ID theorists, because life shows "irreducible complexity," and blind law—especially the Darwinian evolutionary theory that depends on natural selection—cannot explain such complexity. Only an intelligence is able to do this.

In [comparative religion or world religion] classes, ID would not be taught as the truth, but as a system to which others subscribe.

Is ID a form of creationism, meaning a form of biblical literalism that takes the early chapters of Genesis as the basis for world history—six days of creation, six thousand years ago, universal flood, and so forth? Not in so many words at all. A creationist's views encompass ID, but an ID supporter might not accept biblical literalism.

In fact, although some ID supporters are literalists, most are not. The leaders of the movement—the retired lawyer Phillip Johnson, the biochemist Michael Behe, and the philosopher and mathematician William Dembski—all believe in a very old earth, and they all embrace some measure (for Behe, particularly, a large measure) of evolution. The point is that none of these people think that natural selection alone—or any natural-law-driven mechanism—can explain everything.

Ties with Creationism

Having made this distinction, however, I do think that ID and creationism have more than a few links. Supposedly, the ID people do not specify what kind of intelligence is involved in getting over the hump of irreducible complexity, but it is pretty clear in their writings that this intelligence is the Christian God. No one thinks that a super-bright grad student on Andromeda is running an experiment here on planet Earth and that every now and then he or she jiggles things about a bit to see what will happen. Dembski, for one, has been explicit that he sees the designing intelligence as the Logos talked of at the beginning of Saint John's Gospel.

I believe that there is an even greater tie between creationism and ID. Both groups worry about right living—"moral values," in today's jargon. Traditional creationists like Henry Morris and Duane T. Gish are explicit "premillennial Dispensationalists," meaning that they think that Jesus is going to return soon, lead the troops at the battle of Armageddon, and then rule the earth for a thousand years before the Last Judgment. This means that all human efforts at progress are pointless. Better to concentrate on personal purity and converting people, so that God will be pleased with you when he returns.

Some ID folk (the philosopher of science, Paul Nelson, for example) share these eschatological views. Most do not. But they do seem to agree with the creationists that moral values are the real issue and that evolution points to a different—a wrong—kind of future.

I argue strongly against teaching ID in biology classes in state-supported schools.

Again and again, ID writings go off on moral crusades—moral crusades in the direction of traditional evangelical Christianity. Johnson particularly is always fulminating against modern society—divorce, single mothers, kids in jail, homosexuality, cross-dressing (a particular Johnson bugaboo), and more.

ID in the Curriculum

Turn now to the second question. Should this sort of stuff be taught in schools? I do expect morality to be taught, or at least I expect the kids to leave school with a sense of moral values. I do not share all of the ID values—I think gays are just regular people—but I recognize that Americans have different values, and I can see that schools should try to reflect this a bit. I do not want everyone in Kansas to come out a bigot, but obviously teachers are going to reflect their societies. Overall, I want teachers to teach children the worth of every human being and the common decencies that go with that realization.

I am quite happy with the teaching of ID in courses on religion—not theology, but comparative religion or world religion. In such classes, ID would not be taught as the truth, but as a system to which others subscribe. Personally, I think that we have a crying need for courses in comparative religion. I want to see various kinds of Christianity covered, but also other religions. In this day and age, I think every American child should have at least a nodding acquaintance with Islam, so that we can know what people in Iraq and Iran and Afghanistan truly believe.

Teaching ID Is Unconstitutional

However, I argue strongly against teaching ID in biology classes in state-supported schools. If people want to do this in privately funded religious schools, well, that is one of the costs of democracy. But state schools are another matter. In 1981, I went down to the State of Arkansas as an expert witness (in the philosophy of science) to aid the ACLU [American Civil Liberties Union] in a successful attempt to beat back a creationism-friendly law. I would do the same today to beat back an ID-friendly law.

Why do I say this? Why should my beliefs—my evolutionary beliefs—be given unique status in biology classes? First, because teaching an essentially religious theory like ID— outside of the "comparative religions" scenario I've described—is illegal. ID is religion carefully disguised as science to get around the Constitution—that is why ID supporters rarely talk explicitly of God—but it is religion nevertheless. If the Supreme Court rules otherwise, then that will not be the first time that the Supreme Court has been wrong.

Teach students about [ID] in comparative religion courses, along with Christian ideas and the ideas of other faiths. But keep it out of biology classes.

More importantly, ID should not be taught because it is not fruitful as science. Saying that the designer did something is what the philosopher Alvin Plantinga has labeled a "science stopper." If you say that someone intervened, then you are stuck about what to do next. The successful scientist, including the scientist who spends all day Sunday on his or her knees in church praying, is a methodological atheist. Science works by assuming blind law and then going out to find it. Putting matters bluntly, today's biologists argue that Darwinian evolutionary theory works; it is well tested; and although there are controversies (for instance, over the paleontological theory of punctuated equilibrium promoted by the late Stephen Jay Gould), the theory is accepted. On the other hand, ID theory adds nothing to our store of knowledge. It is promoted only because people have religious beliefs they hold dear, and that is simply not the basis for good science.

Teaching the Best You Have

But what about the argument that students should be allowed to decide for themselves? Put both Darwinism and ID on the exam, and do not penalize a student for opting for one over the other? With all due respect to the president, that is nonsense. Good education is not a matter of indifferently offering to students a range of options—a kind of intellectual smorgasbord—and then letting them choose. Good education is teaching the best that you have, together with the critical skills to take inquiry further—perhaps indeed overturning everything that we hold dear. If I heard that my university's med students had to take time out from surgery or pharmacology in order to learn the principles of faith healing or witch-doctoring, because some people believe in them, I would be appalled—and so would you.

So, I say: ID is religion. It is Creationism Lite. Teach students about it in comparative religion courses, along with Christian ideas and the ideas of other faiths. But keep it out of biology classes. It has no proper place in them.

11

Outlawing Discussion of Intelligent Design in Schools Is a Violation

John H. Calvert

John H. Calvert, a lawyer, is managing director of the Intelligent Design Network Inc. Calvert, who counsels school boards, school administrators, and science teachers regarding the teaching of origins science, is co-author of Intelligent Design: The Scientific Alternative to Evolution.

Policies that endorse the teaching of material causes for life and forbid teaching alternative evidence of intelligent design violate Constitutional neutrality by favoring one religion over another. The materialist, non-theistic world view that supports evolution is as much a religion as world views that believe life was created by God or gods. To censor scientific evidence that supports a theistic world view and that contradicts a non-theistic world view violates the principle of scientific objectivity. Indeed, endorsing evolution alone is, essentially, state sponsorship of materialism.

The twisted decision of the court in Dover, PA on December 21 [2005] effectively establishes a state sponsored ideology that is fundamental to non-theistic religions and religious beliefs. By outlawing discussion of the evidence of design and the inference of design that arises from observation and analysis, the court has effectively caused the state to endorse materialism and the various religions it supports. Thus the court actually inserted a religious bias into science, while purporting to remove one.

John H. Calvert, "Dover Court Establishes State Materialism," *The Watchman*, vol. 3, February 2006. Reproduced by permission of the author.

The incorrect assumption implicit in the decision is that there is only one kind of "religion"—the kind that holds that life and the world were created by a God or gods. In fact religion includes the other kinds, those that embrace material causes for life rather than any God that might intervene in the natural world. These include Atheism, Secular Humanism, Buddhism, Agnosticism, etc. The court's second error was to ignore the obvious: any explanation of origins will *unavoidably* favor one kind of religion over another.

A Key Judicial Mistake

For Judge [John] Jones "religion" seems to be a term that describes only belief in a God. Although the judge was quick to note the theistic friendly implications of an intelligent cause for life, his opinion omits any discussion of the religious implications of materialism, the opposite of the idea that life may be the product of an intelligent, rather than a material cause. Materialism is the root of evolution's core claim that life is not designed because it claims to be adequately explained via material causes. Instead he arrives at the absurd conclusion that evolutionary theory "in no way conflicts with, nor does it deny, the existence of a divine creator." This key mistake of the court was caught by an ardent opponent of ID and philosopher of science, Daniel Dennett, who said after the decision:

> I must say that I find that claim to be disingenuous. The theory of evolution demolishes the best reason anyone has ever suggested for believing in a divine *creator*. This does not demonstrate that there *is no* divine creator, of course, but only shows that if there is one, it (He?) needn't have bothered to create anything, since natural selection would have taken care of all that. . . .

This mistake is crucial to the outcome of the case. By ignoring the major competing religious implications of evolutionary theory and materialism/naturalism he has effectively caused the state to prefer one kind of religion over another, the very antithesis of constitutional neutrality.

The court also failed to discuss the fact that the inference of design derives from an observation and logical and rational analysis of the data, not from a religious text. Nor does he discuss or ask, from whence does a counter-intuitive inference of "no-design" arise? From the data or from a philosophy? He makes it clear that it derives from a philosophy: "methodological naturalism." Which hypothesis is truly inferential and scientific? Which idea arises from the data and which from philosophy?

Censoring Evidence

Evolution, and methodological naturalism which effectively shields it from scientific criticism, is key to all of the major non-theistic religions and belief systems. The Dover opinion censors scientific data that is friendly to one set of religious beliefs in favor of data that supports competing and antagonistic belief systems. For the court, it is OK for the state to put into the minds of impressionable students evidence that promotes a materialistic and non-theistic world view while censoring contradictory evidence that supports a theistic one. How can teaching only one side of this scientific controversy be secular, neutral and non-ideological?

A ruling that effectively insulates evolution from scientific criticism actually converts it into an ideology. It takes the theory out of the realm of science and makes it a religion in and of itself. Unfortunately, the court fails to recognize that the only way for the state to deal with the unavoidable religious problem entailed by any discussion of "*Where do we come from?*" is to objectively provide students with relevant scientific information on both sides of that controversy. As soon as the state takes sides in that discussion it steps over the wall.

A Lack of Objectivity

On December 21, 2005, the court in Dover caused the state to take sides in that religiously charged discussion. Four days before Christmas, the court in Dover instituted state sponsorship of materialism.

The 139-page opinion shows a remarkable lack of understanding of other issues critical to the decision. Rather than seek a true understanding of evolution, intelligent design, the scientific method and methodological naturalism, the court accepted hook, line and sinker the propaganda of true "Fundamentalists," who are as passionate about their "Fundamentalism" as those of the Dover Board. The court ignored key evidence that challenges evolution's claim that life is not designed. It called a strike when the ball hit the dirt six feet in front of the batter.

True institutional scientific objectivity is the only antidote to this religious problem. There is no issue in science that cries out more for competing hypotheses than highly subjective "historical narratives" about our origins. From where we come is inseparable from where we go. So long as only one answer to this question is allowed the story will necessarily be religious. We need the competition to make the explanations truly scientific.

The decision in Dover took evolution out of science and made it a religion. I have confidence that this truth will eventually emerge and be corrected.

12

Intelligent Design Movement Undermines Separation of Church and State

Barbara Carroll Forrest

Barbara Carroll Forrest, professor of philosophy at Southeastern Louisiana University, serves on the board of directors of the National Science Education. She is co-author of Creationism's Trojan Horse: The Wedge of Intelligent Design *and was a controversial expert witness for the plaintiffs in* Kitzmiller v. Dover Area School District, *in which Judge John Jones barred the district from teaching intelligent design.*

The goal of the intelligent design (ID) movement is to chip away at the separation of church and state. ID advocates hope to undermine science education by invoking God as a scientific explanation for natural phenomena. To get around the prohibition against teaching creationism in public schools, ID proponents argue that ID theory is simply an alternative to evolutionary theory. They do not, however, provide any scientific evidence to support this claim. ID's ultimate goal—to hold out Christianity as the truth and secular and other beliefs as falsehoods—violates the secularism and religious tolerance that are necessary to democracy.

In *Creationism's Trojan Horse*, Paul R. Gross and I explained the nature and strategy of the intelligent design (ID) creationist movement, which is headquartered at the Discovery

Barbara Carroll Forrest, "Inside Creationism's Trojan Horse: A Closer Look at Intelligent Design," *Georgia Journal of Science*, vol. 63, Fall 2005, pp. 153–62. Copyright 2005 Georgia Academy of Science. Reproduced by permission.

Institute (DI), a conservative think tank in Seattle, WA. In 1996, DI established the Center for the Renewal of Science and Culture (CRSC), now called the Center for Science and Culture (CSC), to promote "intelligent design theory." Functioning as DI's creationist arm, the CSC is advancing a religious agenda by cultivating political influence with state boards of education, local school boards, and members of Congress. Executing a twenty-year plan outlined in a document called "The Wedge Strategy" (a.k.a. the "Wedge Document"), ID creationists hope to drive a "wedge" between the concept of science and the naturalistic methodology by which science operates. This would foster in the public mind a pre-modern understanding of science in which God is invoked as a scientific explanation of natural phenomena. An early CRSC website announced that "new developments in biology, physics, and artificial intelligence are raising serious doubts about scientific materialism and re-opening the case for the supernatural." ID proponents call this "theistic science." ...

Wedge leaders deny that ID is religion and, consequently, that it is creationism. Most worrisome is [Stephen C.] Meyer's contention that the 1987 U.S. Supreme Court ruling, *Edwards v. Aguillard*, which outlawed creationism in public school science classes, "does not apply to design theory" since ID is science. Claiming that "intelligent design fits the bill as a full-scale scientific revolution," [William] Dembski challenges critics: "Ask any leader in the intelligent design movement whether intelligent design is stealth creationism, and they'll deny it." Yet their own words show that ID is characterized by that hallmark of creationism, the rejection of evolution in favor of creation by a supernatural deity. [Phillip E.] Johnson has stated flatly, "Evolution is a hoax." "Darwinism is not science," insists [Michael] Behe. DI president Bruce Chapman promotes the falsehood that "Darwinism is a theory in crisis." And Dembski identifies ID as not only a religious but a sectarian Christian belief: "Intelligent design is just the Logos theology of John's Gospel restated in the idiom of information theory." . . .

ID Is Not Science

A telling piece of evidence that ID is not science is the total failure by Wedge scientists to produce original research supporting ID—even by Behe, a practicing biochemist who claims to have embraced ID for scientific rather than religious reasons. Declining to discuss ID at scientific meetings—"I just don't think that large scientific meetings are effective forums for presenting these ideas"—he chooses instead to discuss it in churches. After thirteen years of the Wedge Strategy (which Johnson says began in 1992 at a conference at Southern Methodist University), Paul Nelson, himself a Wedge founder (and young-earth creationist), recently assessed ID's current scientific status:

> "Science in the Key of Design" if you will, is a melody that we're going to have to teach others to hear and play. First, of course, we have to master it ourselves! . . .

> Easily the biggest challenge facing the ID community is to develop a full-fledged theory of biological design. We don't have such a theory right now, and that's a real problem. Without a theory, it's very hard to know where to direct your research focus. Right now, we've got a bag of powerful intuitions, and a handful of notions such as "irreducible complexity" and "specified complexity"—but, as yet, no general theory of biological design. . . .

Disguising ID's Aims

In the Wedge's early years, ID creationists candidly displayed their true identity and agenda; they needed to raise money and cultivate their support base, which the Wedge Document calls ID's "natural constituency, namely, Christians." They did not shy away from the word "creationist" and were forthright in their references to the supernatural. However, as they have assumed a higher public profile, they have adopted euphemisms to disguise their aims to mainstream audiences (although they drop their linguistic façade when addressing religious supporters). . . . In the wake of publications exposing ID's religious foundations and political ambitions, they have strategically altered their terminology, attempting to conceal their identity as creationists. But their code words are clearly identifiable.

The rejection of naturalism is merely a backhanded way of arguing that an appeal to the supernatural can suffice as a scientific explanation.

One ID tactic is to try to convince school boards to alter the way evolution is taught, as Darby, Montana, minister Curtis Brickley did in 2004. Brickley's proposal to add "intelligent design" to Darby's high school science curriculum was supported by three of five school board members. Both [John] Calvert and CSC fellow David K. DeWolf, a law professor, addressed the board on Brickley's behalf. After opposition by Ravalli County Citizens for Science (RCCS), Brickley altered his terminology, requesting the teaching of "objective origins" rather than "intelligent design." RCCS ultimately won: a new board scuttled the policy after the next election. But ID activity continues in other states, and ID code talk includes a variety of other euphemisms.

The ID movement has a more ominous side: its leaders attack the secularism and religious tolerance that are vital to constitutional democracy.

Creating a Controversy in Science

The CSC promotes "teaching the controversy," hoping to convince the public and educational policymakers that there is a raging debate over evolution in mainstream science. Stymied so far in efforts to get ID into science classes via the front door, ID creationists take the backdoor approach of proposing that the "strengths and weaknesses of evolution" be taught in order to encourage "critical thinking" or, as in the Ohio benchmark and lesson plan, "critical analysis." They used the "strengths and weaknesses" approach in an unsuccessful attempt to influence the Texas Board of Education's selection of science textbooks in 2003. ID creationists yet needed another euphemism for their attempt to evade the legal constraints of *Edwards v. Aguillard*, in which the U.S. Supreme Court outlawed creationism while acknowledging that "teaching a variety of scientific theories about the origins of humankind to schoolchildren might be validly done with the clear secular intent of enhancing the effectiveness of science instruction". Viewing this as a legal loophole, ID creationists pronounced ID an "alternative theory," a scientific competitor to evolutionary theory. Even further, co-opting the language of civil liberties to disguise their reactionary agenda, they argue that teaching ID is protected by "a teacher's right to academic freedom." One of the most effective terms in the ID lexicon is "fairness," used in constant appeals to allow children to hear "both sides" of ID's contrived controversy. According to Dembski, one of ID's favorite tactics is "to appeal to the undecided middle's sense of fairness and justice, especially its tendency to root for the underdog and its predilection for freedom of expression." But the ID tactic that most conclusively identifies ID as religion is its rejection of "naturalism."

ID's anti-naturalism is central to the Wedge Strategy. Johnson conflates "methodological naturalism," which is simply a fancy name for scientific method, with "philosophical naturalism," a metaphysical view that reaches beyond science in its conclusion that the supernatural does not exist. Johnson wrongly but deliberately equates these terms in order to argue that teaching evolution, the product of science's naturalistic methodology, is tantamount to teaching atheism in public school science classes. But his rejection of naturalism is merely a backhanded way of arguing that an appeal to the supernatural can suffice as a scientific explanation. In doing so, Johnson ignores the essential distinction between science and religion that constitutes an elementary understanding of science. . . .

The aggressive [ID] campaign . . . points to a troubled future for public education and constitutional democracy.

Attacking Religious Tolerance

In addition to its religiously motivated anti-evolutionism, the ID movement has a more ominous side: its leaders attack the secularism and religious tolerance that are vital to constitutional democracy. CSC fellow Benjamin Wiker asserts that ID "directly contradicts the modern secularist intellectual trend that has so thoroughly dominated Western culture for the last two centuries." He warns, "Soon enough, secularized culture will be compelled to re-align." Dembski and Johnson promote a disturbing religious exclusionism. Displaying a penchant for military metaphors, Dembski calls ID "ground zero of the culture war." By his own admission, Christian apologetics (the defense of Christianity against perceived attacks) forms the foundation of his work as a "design theorist." For Dembski, ID goes hand-in-hand with an aggressive forward movement into [a] secular society by defenders of Christian orthodoxy: "We are to engage the secular world, reproving, rebuking and exhorting it, pointing to the truth of Christianity." Christianity, he says, has a "dark side" for "those who refuse to embrace this truth." He favors reviving the religious transgression of heresy: "Heresy remains a valid category for today." Knowing that his Christian "mandate" will be unpopular, he asks rhetorically, "Can't we all just get along and live together in peace?" His reply is chilling: "Unfortunately, the answer is no." . . .

The religious exclusionism of ID leaders has at times taken on another facet: the criticism of non-Christian religious belief. In an interview about the ID movement with *Christianity Today*, Johnson, referring to [the terrorist attacks in the United States [on September 11, 2001], spoke in the same breath of Muslim terrorists and Muslim students in American universities. He implied that Muslims worship a false god:

> Now we're seeing how the country is almost cringing in fear of these Muslim terrorists from the Middle East. I see professors afraid to discuss the subject because they're afraid of what the Muslim students will do. They're afraid it won't keep the peace on campus. I never thought our country would descend to this level. We are afraid to search [for] the truth and to proclaim it. We once knew who the true God was and were able to proclaim it frankly.

In promoting ID for more than a decade, Johnson has repeatedly stressed his desire to move the country back toward what he considers its Christian foundation. Given his role as the catalyst for the formation of the Wedge and the sectarian Christian foundation upon which he and his fellow Wedge members have built their movement, such exclusionary sentiments can be understood as an integral part of the ID edifice.

Journalists have asked me how the Discovery Institute creationists, all well-educated and some with scientific credentials, can truly believe what they tell the public and educational policymakers about ID's purported scientific validity and evolution's impending demise. Although such puzzlement is inevitable if ID is isolated from its cultural, religion, and political framework, the ID movement is not puzzling at all when one views it within this context. It must be understood as part of something more than a strategy dreamed up by a relative handful of well-financed religious zealots: it is another column in the Religious Right's attack on public education and secular society, and the Wedge Strategy constitutes ID's logistical contribution to this attack. The aggressive campaign waged for more than a dozen years now [between 1993 and 2005] by Wedge members and their supporters points to a troubled future for public education and constitutional democracy. Citizens who value both should understand what the ID agenda portends. . . .

The long-term results of ID proponents' coordinated actions against teaching evolution, with the consequent diversion of time and money toward fending off its advances, will be the deterioration of science education, already threatened in many places by under-prepared and intimidated teachers. Fewer students who are properly educated about science will translate into fewer students who are qualified to become scientists. And the results of ID's encroachment upon the public policy-making process include the further erosion of secular democracy, the bulwark of academic freedom that is the lifeblood of science. Separation of church and state may appear only distantly related to science education—until one remembers that we have only one Constitution to protect both. Science education is ID's chosen vehicle for its role in the Religious Right's broader attack on secular society. The undermining of church and state separation will mean the undermining of science education as well.

13

Overcoming Public Acceptance of Intelligent Design by the Scientific Method

Scott O. Lilienfeld

Scott O. Lilienfeld, professor of psychology at Emory University, is co-editor of Science and Pseudoscience in Clinical Psychology.

The public has embraced intelligent design (ID) because it is more plausible to believe that an intelligent designer created the complex biological structures that flourish in the natural world than to believe that they were created by mutation and natural selection. However, human senses are often misleading. People believed that the Sun revolved around Earth until scientists proved otherwise. To overcome belief in the plausibility of pseudoscience and intelligent design, schools must teach the fallibility of the human senses and the purpose of the scientific method, which is to safeguard against human error.

The growing popularity of intelligent design (ID) has left most scientists baffled, even exasperated. From their perspective, the match-up between Darwin's theory of natural selection and ID would be laughable were it not so worrisome. It pits one theory backed by tens of thousands of peer-reviewed articles and consistent with multiple lines of converging genetic, physiological, and paleontological evidence

Scott O. Lilienfeld, "Why Scientists Shouldn't Be Surprised by the Popularity of Intelligent Design," *Skeptical Inquirer*, vol. 30, no. 3, May–June 2006, pp. 46–9. Copyright 2006 Committee for the Scientific Investigation of Claims of the Paranormal. Reproduced by permission.

against an armchair conjecture that has flown under the radar of peer review and has yet to generate a single confirmed scientific prediction. If the contest were a boxing match, the referee would surely have stopped the fight seconds after the opening bell.

Embracing ID

Yet, to the dismay of most scientists, large swaths of the American public not only harbor serious doubts about Darwinian theory but believe that ID should be taught in science classes. In a 2005 Gallup poll, 34 percent of Americans said they believed that Darwinian theory was false and 31 percent favored ID as an explanation for the development of species. As of this writing [May–June 2006] at least forty states are considering initiatives to include ID in public school science curricula. [In November 2005] the Kansas Board of education voted to adopt standards mandating teachers to raise questions about Darwinian theory. Echoing the language of ID advocates, these standards refer to unexplained gaps in the fossil record and other purported challenges to the scientific status of this theory. [On December 21, 2005], U.S. District Judge John Jones ruled that ID could not be taught as an alternative to Darwinian theory in Dover, Pennsylvania, public schools. . . .

In response to such developments, many scientists have expressed disdain—even ridicule—for believers in ID. Nobel Prize winner James D. Watson, co-discoverer of the structure of DNA, was quoted recently in the *New York Times* as saying that only people who "put their common sense on hold" doubt evolutionary theory. Still other scientists have attributed malevolent intent to ID advocates. Expressing bewilderment at the ascendance of ID among the American public, one of my academic psychology colleagues abroad recently asked me, "What has happened to good sense and decency in the USA?"

Nevertheless, from the standpoint of psychological science, the only thing about ID's popularity that should surprise us is that so many scientists are surprised by it. Of course, much of the resistance to Darwinian theory is theological, and media coverage of ID proponents has accorded nearly exclusive emphasis to the intimate connection between ID and fundamentalist Christianity. Nevertheless, religion doesn't tell the whole story.

Standing in the way of the public's acceptance of evolutionary theory . . . is the public's erroneous belief that common sense is a dependable guide to evaluating the natural world.

ID's Compatibility with Intuition

The other reason for the public's embrace of intelligent design is its compatibility with intuition. *Contra* Watson, it is Darwinian evolution, not ID, that is glaringly inconsistent with common sense. Political commentator Patrick J. Buchanan's (2005) statements are illustrative in this regard. Invoking "common sense," "experience," and "reason," Buchanan asked rhetorically, "How can evolution explain the creation of that extraordinary instrument, the human eye?"

Indeed, from the vantage point of commonplace intuition, it is far more plausible to believe that complex biological structures like the peacock's tail and elephant's trunk were shaped by a teleological force than by purposeless processes of mutation and natural selection operating over millions of years. To many laypeople, the latter explanation seems hopelessly farfetched. ID theorists have capitalized on this "argument from personal incredulity," as biologist Richard Dawkins terms it, using the sculpted presidential faces on Mount Rushmore as a thought experiment. If an alien visiting the earth were to happen upon these faces, they ask, would it regard them as the outcome of intentional design or of unguided physical processes? The answer is obvious.

The foremost obstacle standing in the way of the public's acceptance of evolutionary theory is not a dearth of common sense. Instead, it is the public's erroneous belief that common sense is a dependable guide to evaluating the natural world. Even some prominent scientists and science writers have missed this crucial point. In a widely discussed article, psychologists Joaquim Krueger of Brown University and David Funder of the University of California-Riverside urged their colleagues to accord more credence to common sense notions of human nature. . . . And in a *New York Times* op-ed, . . . science writer John Horgan called for a heightened emphasis on common sense in the evaluation of scientific theories.

The Problem with Common Sense

Yet natural science is replete with hundreds of examples demonstrating that common sense is frequently misleading. The world seems flat rather than round. The sun seems to revolve around Earth rather than vice-versa. Objects in motion seem to slow down on their own accord, when in fact they remain in motion unless opposed by a countervailing force.

[Scientists] must teach students . . . why researchers developed scientific methods in the first place, namely as an essential safeguard against human error.

In my own discipline of psychology, striking violations of our intuitions abound. Memory seems to operate like a video camera or tape recorder, but research demonstrates that memory is fallible and reconstructive. Most people believe that shifty eyes are good indicators of lying, but research reveals otherwise. Many people believe that opposites attract in relationships, but research shows that opposites tend to repel. The same goes for scores of other common sense claims regarding human nature, such as the belief that expressing anger is typically better than holding it in, that raising children in similar ways leads to marked similarities in their personalities, that most physically abused children grow up to become abusers themselves, and that the levels of psychiatric hospital admissions, crimes, and suicides increase markedly during full moons.

Of course, none of this demonstrates that common sense is worthless. When it comes to gauging our long-term emotional preferences for people and products, research suggests that we are often better off trusting our gut hunches than engaging in dry, objective analyses of the pros and cons. Yet when it comes to discerning the workings of the outside world or the three-pound world inside of our cranial cavities, common sense is an exceedingly undependable barometer of the truth.

Ironically, if scientists took the implications of evolutionary theory more seriously, they would understand why. The human brain evolved to increase the probability that the genes of the body it inhabits make their way into subsequent generations. It did not evolve to infer general principles about the operation of the natural world, let alone to understand itself. It also did not evolve to comprehend vast expanses of time, such as the unimaginable tens or hundreds of millions of years over which biological systems evolved. Consequently, it is hardly surprising that many intelligent individuals, like Patrick Buchanan, glance at the remarkably intricate biological world and conclude that it must have been produced by a designer.

Teaching the Scientific Method

To a substantial extent, the fault in the current ID wars lies not with the general public, but with scientists and science educators themselves. Generations of biology, chemistry, and physics instructors have taught their disciplines largely as collections of disembodied findings and facts. Rarely have they emphasized the importance of the scientific method as an essential toolbox of skills designed to prevent us from fooling ourselves. As Alan Cromer and Lewis Wolpert have noted, science does not come naturally to any of us, because it often requires us to think in ways that run counter to our common sense. Mark Twain observed that education requires us to unlearn old habits at least as much as learn new ones. Nowhere is Twain's maxim truer than in effective science education, which asks us to unlearn our reflexive inclination to uncritically trust our perceptions.

Unless scientists institute a fundamental change in how science is taught, it may be only a matter of time before a new and even more virulent variant of Intelligent Design emerges.

Moreover, scientists and the skeptical community at large have long been waging the battle against pseudoscience on only a single front. They have treated each dubious claim, whether it be ID, astrology, or the latest quack herbal remedy, as an isolated thinking error to be combated. In doing so, they have fogotten that the popularity of ID is merely one example of a far broader problem, namely the American public's embrace of pseudoscience in its myriad incarnations. This one-claim-at-a-time approach helps to explain why scientists are losing not only the ID wars, but also the broader war against public belief in pseudoscience. About a quarter of Americans believe that astrology is scientific and about half believe in extrasensory perception despite the virtually wholesale absence of evidence for either assertion. Public acceptance of alternative medicine continues to mount despite controlled studies showing that most popular alternative remedies are ineffective. Slaying each pseudoscientific dragon as it emerges is laudable and at times necessary, but as a long-term strategy against irrationality it is destined to fail.

The Battle Against Pseudoscience

Indeed, to win the long-term battle against pseudoscience, scientists must look beyond the narrow battles against ID. The real war they must wage is in the classroom. Specifically, scientists need to effect a sea-change in how science is taught at the junior high, high school, and college levels. They must teach students not merely the core knowledge of their subject matter, but also an understanding of why researchers developed scientific methods in the first place, namely as an essential safeguard against human error.

To do so, they must inculcate in students a profound sense of humility regarding their own perceptions and interpretations of the world. They should teach students about optical illusions, which demonstrate that our perceptions can mislead us. They should show students how their common sense notions regarding the movements of physical objects, like the trajectory of a ball emerging from a spiral, are often incorrect. They should teach students that even highly confident eyewitness reports are frequently inaccurate. Most broadly, they must counteract what Stanford psychologist Lee Ross calls "naïve realism"—the deeply ingrained notion that what we see invariably reflects the true state of nature.

Scientists may well emerge victorious from the current ID battles. Given that the research evidence is overwhelmingly on their side, they certainly deserve to. Yet as Dawkins reminds us, ideas can mutate at least as readily as genes. Unless scientists institute a fundamental change in how science is taught, it may be only a matter of time before a new and even more virulent variant of Intelligent Design emerges. Then scientists will again be surprised at the public's uncritical embrace of it, while shaking their heads in disbelief at the average American's lack of common sense.

14

Critics Should Not Fear Questions About Intelligent Design or Evolution

J. Scott Turner

J. Scott Turner, professor of biology at the State University of New York's College of Environmental Science and Forestry, is author of the Tinkerer's Accomplice: How Design Emerges from Life Itself.

One of the best ways to give credence to a false idea is to censor it. If Darwinists refuse to allow people to ask questions about evolution, they should not be surprised if the rest of the world wonders why they are unwilling to do so. In fact, answering questions about evolution will improve our understanding of it. Moreover, critics of intelligent design should welcome debate. Indeed, academia is the appropriate place to discuss ideas, good or bad.

I'd never had a heckler before. Usually, when I'm asked to give a talk, I discuss my research on termites and the remarkable structures they build. Usually, I'm glad just to have an audience. But what I'd learned from termites had got me thinking about broader issues, among them the question of design in biology: Why are living things built so well for the functions they perform? So I wrote a book called *The Tinkerer's Accomplice*, which was my topic that day.

The trouble started almost as soon as I stepped up to the podium: intrusive "questions" and demands for "clarifica-

J. Scott Turner, "Why Can't We Discuss Intelligent Design?" *Chronicle of Higher Education*, January 19, 2007, p. B20. Copyright © 2007 by The Chronicle of Higher Education. Reprinted with permission of the author.

tions," really intended not to illuminate but to disrupt and distract. In exasperation, I finally had to ask the heckler to give me a chance to make my argument and my audience a chance to hear it, after which he could ask all the questions he wished.

He was not interested in that approach, of course, and left as soon as question time began. I found out later that he'd complained at his next faculty meeting that the departmental speaker's program should never be used as a forum for advancing—what precisely? That was never quite clear, either to me or to my embarrassed host.

Suggesting Design in Nature

I think what stirred up the heckler had something to do with the word "design." Unless clearly linked to the process of natural selection, "design" can be a bit of a red flag for modern biologists. The reason is not hard to fathom. Most people, when they contemplate the living world, get an overwhelming sense that it is a designed place, replete with marvelous and ingenious contrivances: the beak of a hummingbird curved like the nectaries it feeds from, bones shaped to the loads they must bear, feathers that could teach new tricks to an aeronautical engineer, the nearly unfathomable complexity of a brain that can see—all built as if someone had designed them.

You might believe ... that [intelligent design] is a wrong-headed idea, but it's hard to see how that alone should disqualify it from academic discourse.

And that, in a nutshell, is the problem. Say "design," and you imply that a designer has been at work, with all the attributes implied by that word: forward-looking, purposeful, intelligent, and intentional. For many centuries, most people drew precisely that conclusion from the designs they thought they saw everywhere in nature.

Charles Darwin was supposed to have put paid to that idea, of course, and ever since his day biologists have considered it gauche to speak of design, or even to hint at purposefulness in nature. Doing so in polite company usually earns you what I call The Pause, the awkward silence that typically follows a faux pas.

Sparking a Spectacle

If just one freighted word like "design" can evoke The Pause, combining two—as in the phrase "intelligent design"—seems to make otherwise sane people slip their moorings. If you enjoy irony, as I do, the spectacle can provide hours of entertainment. I wonder, for example, what demon had gripped a past president of Cornell University when he singled out intelligent design as a unique threat to academic and civil discourse. Aren't universities supposed to be a place for dangerous ideas?

Also amusing is the spectacle of independent-minded scientists' running to college administrators or the courts for help in defining what is science and what is permissible discourse in their classrooms. And I find it hard to suppress a chuckle at the sheer brass of books like Richard Dawkins's recent *The God Delusion*, which seem untroubled by traditional boundaries between religion and science as long as the intrusion is going their way.

Faced with all that hue and cry, I almost want to say: "Friends, intelligent design is just an idea." You might believe (as I do) that it is a wrongheaded idea, but it's hard to see how that alone should disqualify it from academic discourse. Academe is full of wrongheaded ideas, and always has been—not because academe itself is wrongheaded, but because to discuss such ideas is its very function. Even bad ideas can contain kernels of truth, and it is academe's role to find them.

That can be done only in the sunlight and fresh air of normal academic discourse. Expelling an idea is the surest way to allow falsehood to survive.

A critic of intelligent design could reasonably reply: "That's all true, but there are limits to how much tolerance should be extended to wrongheadedness. Once falsehood is exposed as such, it needs to be shown the door." It's worth remembering, though, that we have been here before. Intelligent design is just the latest eruption of a longstanding strain of anti-Darwinist thought, which includes the Scopes "monkey" trial of the 1920s, the "creation science" controversies of the 1970s, and many other skirmishes, large and small.

It's hard to see how asking [questions about intelligent design] could do anything but enrich our understanding about evolution and how we teach it.

Questions Worth Pondering

The strain's very persistence invites the obvious question: If Darwin settled the issue once and for all, why does it keep coming back? Perhaps the fault lies with Darwin's supporters. Rather than debate the strain on its merits, we scramble to the courts or the political ramparts to expel it from our classrooms and our students' minds.

That is a pity because at the core of intelligent design is a question worth pondering: Is evolution shaped in any way by purposefulness or intentionality? Darwinism is clear in its answer—no way, no how—and that is not mere obstinacy, as some might charge. The banishment of purpose from evolution is Darwinism's *sine qua non*, which Darwin himself fought hard to establish, and which his descendants have defended stoutly ever since.

Most of the challenges to Darwinism over the years, including intelligent design, have arisen over what most people see as a self-evident link between design and purpose in the living world. A Darwinist would say that the purpose is only *apparent*, that what we believe to be design is actually the accumulated product of an unintentional process of "tinkering," using materials at hand to cobble together solutions to immediate problems—keeping those that work, discarding those that do not, but proceeding with no view of the future, only with the legacy of the past.

But what if evolution really is purposeful in some way? In fact Darwin dethroned only one type of purposefulness, the Platonic idealism that had previously underscored the concept of the species. There's more to purpose than Plato, however, and it remains an open question how other forms of purposefulness might inform our thinking about evolution. What might purposeful evolution look like? Is design its signature? Can it be reconciled with Darwinism? If so, how? If not, why not?

It's hard to see a threat in asking such questions. Indeed, it's hard to see how asking them could do anything but enrich our understanding about evolution and how we teach it.

Here is where I have to give the proponents of intelligent design their (limited) due. Their intellectual pedigree might be suspect, their thinking might be wrong, but at least they are asking an interesting question: What is the meaning of design of the living world?

In our readiness to proscribe intelligent design, we Darwinists are telling the world not only that we are unwilling to ask such questions ourselves, but that we don't want others to ask them either. No wonder the war on Darwin won't go away.

15

Proponents of Intelligent Design Misrepresent Scientists to Support Claims

Jason Rosenhouse

Jason Rosenhouse, an opponent of intelligent design and pseudo-science, is professor of mathematics at James Madison University, in Harrisonburg, Virginia. He is author of the EvolutionBlog and essays, including "How Anti-Evolutionists Abuse Mathematics" and "How Do ID Proponents Behave when Preaching to the Choir?"

One of the reasons many scientists are so intense in their opposition to intelligent design (ID) is that ID advocates often level false charges against evolution and misrepresent scientists to do so. ID proponents will quote scientists in ways that make them appear to question evolutionary theory when these scientists are, in fact, passionate defenders. While scientists can easily identify the misrepresentations and false claims made by ID activists, laypeople do not always have access to all the facts, which explains why ID advocates prefer to present their case to the general public rather than professionals.

I am sometimes asked why supporters of evolution get so angry when addressing proponents of Intelligent Design (ID). My answer is that if the evolution/ID dispute were simply a discussion of rival scientific claims, say about whether

Jason Rosenhouse, "Why Scientists Get so Angry when Dealing with ID Proponents," *Skeptical Inquirer*, vol. 29, November–December, 2005, pp. 42–5. Copyright 2005 Committee for the Scientific Investigation of Claims of the Paranormal. Reproduced by permission.

known evolutionary mechanisms are capable of explaining the formation of complex systems, then the discussion would be far less acrimonious. In reality, however, ID proponents spend most of their time leveling bogus charges against evolution. Professionals in the relevant fields possess the expertise to immediately recognize that the charges are scientifically untrue, but the lay audiences to which these charges are directed are unlikely to be similarly equipped. The result is that ID proponents present a picture of modern biology that is completely unsupported scientifically and disingenuous. And this is why ID proponents are so reviled by scientists.

An Example of ID Duplicity

In this article, I will document one specific example of blatant ID duplicity. It provides a useful study of ID proponents' tactics.

One of the most prolific ID proponents is William Dembski. On April 26, 2005, he published an essay at his blog in which he addressed the charge that ID proponents present quotations inaccurately. The essay began this way:

> Unlike the serious sciences (e.g., quantum electrodynamics, which is accurate up to 14 decimal places), evolution has become an exercise in filling holes by digging others. Fortunately, the cognitive dissonance associated with this exercise can't be suppressed indefinitely, so occasionally evolutionists fess-up that some gaping hole really is there and can't be filled simply by digging another hole. Such admissions, of course, provide ready material for evolution critics like me. Indeed, it's one of the few pleasures in this business sticking it to the evolutionists when they make some particularly egregious admission. Consider the following admission by Peter Ward (Ward is a well-known expert on ammonite fossils and does not favor a ID-based view)....

Dembski is about to present a quotation from paleontologist Peter Ward to support his contention that there are gaping holes in evolutionary biology. Dembski tells us that the quotation he is about to present is the product of the cognitive dissonance created when scientists must suppress what they know to be true about the deficiencies of evolution.

We will come to the quotation in a moment, but first there is some history to recount. As described by Dembski, he first used Ward's statement in an essay entitled "Five Questions Evolutionists Would Rather Dodge," posted at his Web site on April 14, 2004. Shortly after this essay was posted, two contributors to "The Panda's Thumb" blog, Gary Hurd and Dave Mullenix, wrote a rebuttal taking Dembski to task for, among other things, misusing Ward's statement. Dembski's blog entry, quoted above, was to be a belated reply to Hurd and Mullenix.

Looking for the Straight Story

Prior to reading Dembski's blog entry [quoted above], I had not read his "Five Questions" essay. Likewise, I had not read the reply by Hurd and Mullenix. I also had never heard of Peter Ward, had not read the book from which the quote was taken, and did not know anything about Ward's scientific opinions. Consequently, I was able to investigate the situation with no preconceived notions about who was telling me the truth. I knew that the facts of the matter would be easy enough to obtain, and that they would allow me to determine who was providing the straight story.

I began by reading Dembski's essay. The relevant statement is the following:

> The challenge that here confronts evolution is not isolated but pervasive, and comes up most flagrantly in what's called the Cambrian Explosion. In a very brief window of time during the geological period known as the Cambrian, virtually all the basic animal types appeared suddenly in the fossil record with no trace of evolutionary ancestors. The Cambrian explosion so flies in the face of evolution that

paleontologist Peter Ward wrote, "If ever there was evidence suggesting Divine Creation, surely the Precambrian and Cambrian transition, known from numerous localities across the face of the earth, is it." Note that Ward is not a creationist.

Already a question emerges. Taken at face value, Ward's statement above seems to affirm the idea that the Cambrian Explosion is strong evidence for Divine Creation. If that is an accurate presentation of Ward's opinion on this subject, then why *isn't* Ward a creationist?

Ward made his statement in his 1992 book *On Methuselah's Trail*. I obtained a copy of the book, flipped to page 29, and found that Ward had indeed written the words being attributed to him. The quoted line comes at the beginning of a ten-page section entitled "The Base of the Cambrian." In this section Ward provides a brief history of what is known about the Precambrian to Cambrian transition.

The Whole Story

So I decided to read the rest of the section. After the line Dembski quoted, Ward goes on to describe Darwin's own concerns about the Cambrian explosion (though that term did not exist in Darwin's time). He also discusses various explanations offered by some of Darwin's contemporaries, such as Roger Murchison and Adam Sedgwick, and shows how those explanations fared in the face of subsequent discoveries.

This goes on for several pages. Eventually Ward comes to more modern views of the subject. And this is where Dembski's creative use of quotations becomes obvious. On page 35, Ward writes this:

> Until almost 1950 the absence of metazoan fossils older than Cambrian age continued to puzzle evolutionists and earth historians alike. Other than the remains of single-celled creatures and the matlike stromatolites, it did indeed

look as if larger creatures had arisen with a swiftness that made a mockery of Darwin's theory of evolution. This notion was finally put to rest, however, by the discovery of the Ediacarian and Vendian fossil faunas of latest Precambrian age.

On page 36 we find:

Intensive searching of strata immediately underlying the well-known basal Cambrian deposits in the years between 1950 and 1980 showed that the larger skeletonized fossils (such as the trilobites and brachiopods) that supposedly appeared so suddenly were in fact preceded by skeletonized forms so small as to be easily overlooked by the pioneering geologists.

Solving the Problem

And just in case there is still any doubt, Ward closes the section with the following statement:

The long-accepted theory of the sudden appearance of skeletal metazoans at the base of the Cambrian was incorrect: the basal Cambrian boundary marked only the first appearance of relatively large skeleton-bearing forms, such as the brachipods and trilobites, rather than the first appearance of skeletonized metazoans. Darwin would have been satisfied. The fossil record bore out his conviction that the trilobites and brachipods appeared only after a long period of evolution of ancestral forms. (pages 36–37)

From these statements it is obvious that Ward does *not* believe the Cambrian explosion is an insoluble problem for evolution. Quite the contrary. He states clearly that recent fossil discoveries pertaining to the Cambrian explosion have been a vindication of Darwin.

So what about that "Divine Creation" remark? In context it is obviously a framing sentence intended to set up the ensuing discussion. Ward was not stating his own opinion or the opinion of any particular modern paleontologist. Instead he was merely describing the way things seemed to many people prior to Darwin, and for many years after Darwin.

The next step was to read what Hurd and Mullenix had to say on this subject. They began with a lengthy discussion in which they showed that Dembski's assertions about the Cambrian explosion, quoted above, are quite false. They next discuss the Ward quote, and come to the same conclusion I did. They even used two of the quotes that I found. They concluded by showing that after distorting Ward's clearly stated intention, Dembski went on to misrepresent a statement from Stephen Jay Gould.

Let's review. Dembski tried to imply that the non-creationist Peter Ward nonetheless agrees with Dembski's view that the Cambrian explosion is a problem for evolution. In reality, Ward's clearly stated view is that while the Cambrian explosion used to be viewed as a problem for evolution, recent fossil discoveries actually show that it is a vindication for Darwin. Hurd and Mullenix pointed this out, showing in great detail that Dembski had not only distorted Ward, but had done likewise to Gould. They also showed that Dembski's version of the facts was simply wrong. Dembski ignored what Hurd and Mullenix had said and repeated his earlier error about Ward's intentions.

Failing to Answer the Real Challenge

And that brings us back to Dembski's blog entry. We resume the action from the point where my opening quote left off. He quotes Ward as saying:

> The seemingly sudden appearance of skeletonized life has been one of the most perplexing puzzles of the fossil record. How is it that animals as complex as trilobites and brachiopods could spring forth so suddenly, completely formed, without a trace of their ancestors in the underlying strata? If ever there was evidence suggesting Divine Creation, surely

the Precambrian and Cambrian transition, known from numerous localities across the face of the earth, is it.

And goes on to say:

Pretty convincing indicator that the Cambrian explosion poses a challenge to conventional evolutionary theory, wouldn't you say? Note that this is not a misquote: I indicate clearly that Ward does not support ID and there's sufficient unedited material here to make clear that he really is saying that the Cambrian explosion poses a challenge to conventional evolutionary theory.

Unlike in his original essay, Dembski now gives the entire paragraph from which the "Divine Creation" statement appeared. Even those few extra sentences are enough to make one suspect that Ward was not saying anything useful to ID folks. The phrases "seemingly" and "has been," suggest that Ward is setting up his readers for the eventual resolution to the problem.

ID proponents are entirely shameless in presenting the most malicious caricatures of modern science.

Dembski asserts that this is not a misquote on the grounds that (a) he indicates clearly that Ward does not support ID and (b) he includes enough material here to show Ward's true intention.

Alas, (a) is totally irrelevant. At issue here is not whether Ward is an evolutionist or a creationist. Rather, the issue is what Ward thinks about the Cambrian explosion. And we have already seen that (b) is false. This paragraph by itself does not reflect Ward's intention. Ward's opinion, as stated in his book, could not have been clearer. This is not a situation where Ward intended one thing, but because of sloppy writing could be plausibly interpreted as saying something else. Nor is this a situation where Ward believes that on balance the evidence supports evolution, but that there are certain holes nonetheless in the current theory.

Creating a Nonexistent Controversy

This is hardly an isolated case. When I first started investigating the evolution/creationism issue I noticed that antievolutionists were constantly quoting scientists in ways that made it appear they had grave reservations about modern theory. I knew for a fact that the people being quoted were themselves passionate defenders of evolution. Initially I found it difficult to understand why these scientists would defend a theory they apparently had deep reservations about.

So I investigated dozens of cases like the one described in this essay. In every case I found that the quotation was badly out of context. Sometimes what was presented as a minor revision of an esoteric part of evolutionary theory was exaggerated into a criticism of the theory as a whole. Other times, like the situation described here, the meaning of a statement was so twisted that it was made to seem to be saying the precise opposite of the author's clearly stated intention. In every case the quotation was made to appear to mean something different from the writer's actual opinion.

This explains why scientists become so angry when dealing with this subject. If the issue were simply that mainstream science says, for example, that current theory is fully capable of accounting for information growth in the genome, while a handful of dissenters claimed otherwise, then I would be all in favor of engaging in polite debate. The reality, however, is that many ID proponents are entirely shameless in presenting the most malicious caricatures of modern science. In response to such behavior, anger is entirely appropriate.

This also explains why ID proponents rarely make any attempt to present their case to professionals. In front of such an audience their distortions would be immediately obvious. They are on far safer ground lobbying school boards and state legislatures. When making your case in front of audiences that do not know the facts of the situation, it is easier to lie with impunity.

16

Christianity and Darwinism Are Not Incompatible

Ted Peters

Ted Peters, who teaches systematic theology at Pacific Lutheran Theological Seminary and the Graduate Theological Union in Berkeley, California, is author of Science, Theology, and Ethics *and co-author of* Evolution from Creation to New Creation: Conflict, Conversation, and Convergence.

Some Christians claim that to believe in the theory of evolution is un-Christian. Correspondingly, some scientists believe that to be religious is to be un-scientific. Neither position is true. Christianity seeks knowledge and understanding of the natural world, and many Christians accept Darwinism as an explanation for the development of life. It is not incompatible with Christianity or science to believe that God's divine purpose was to use evolution to create life.

In the dust storm kicked up by proponents of "Intelligent Design" over what should be taught in the public schools, the science of evolutionary biology—the Darwinian model of evolution—is dubbed as materialistic, reductionistic, and atheistic. The Intelligent Design advocates suggest that to be a Christian one must take a stand against Darwinism. According to them, to pursue scientific research under the principles of

Ted Peters, "Intelligent Religion: Are Science and Faith Really Incompatible?" *Sojourners Magazine*, vol. 34, December, 2005, p. 9. Copyright © 2005 Sojourners. Reprinted with permission from Sojourners. (800) 714-7474, www.sojo.net/index.cfm?action =magazine.article&issue=soj0512&article=051241c.

random variation and natural selection is un-Christian. So-called "theistic evolutionists" (a phrase actually coined by the creationists as a term of derision) are accused of selling out to the enemy.

In turn the scientific establishment tries to assert that to be religious is like having a disease that quarantines a person against participation in science. To accuse someone of holding a religious view about evolution helps to defend the hegemony of the Darwinian model in the public schools. Why? Because science is not subject to First Amendment proscriptions, while religion is. So, if you label your opponents "religious," you get the courts on your side.

The implication is that those who continue to believe in religious things are simply not smart enough to advance. When they become smart, they'll drop their religion and join the scientific community.

It's very possible that one could embrace the science of the Darwinian tradition and also embrace a Christian understanding of God at work in the natural world.

Intelligent Design proponents and creationists insist that the Darwinists are blinded by their atheism so they cannot see the limitations and gaps in their theory. These advocates argue that the very existence of complexity contradicts the standard theory of evolution, which assumes that change occurred gradually, slowly, step by step. They say that a qualitative leap to a higher order of complexity must be acknowledged and that only an appeal to a transcendent intelligent designer provides an adequate explanation. Without quite using the word "stupid," intelligent design advocates suggest that insistence by Darwinists that natural selection suffices as an explanation shows at least a lack of open-mindedness.

The Theistic Evolutionists

What all of this leaves out is my group of friends and colleagues. I hang out with those so-called theistic evolutionists. We tend to think scientists are pretty smart. In fact, many of my colleagues are research scientists, even evolutionary biologists. We are convinced that the neo-Darwinian model of random genetic variation combined with natural selection provides the most adequate explanation for the development of life forms.

But my friends and colleagues are also religious, mostly Christian but with some other faiths mixed in. We think religious people can be pretty smart too. What is so important and what gets missed too often when the media covers the evolution wars is this: To be a Christian does not require that one be anti-Darwinian.

It's very possible that one could embrace the science of the Darwinian tradition and also embrace a Christian understanding of God at work in the natural world. I believe that God has used the evolution of life over deep time to serve a divine purpose for creation. This requires distinguishing between the strictly scientific Darwinian model and the atheism and related ideologies that have frequently been associated with evolution. The science is solid.

Christian faith seeks understanding, as St. Anselm put it. Historically, Christians have fallen in love with science. Faith loves science. Today, the Christian faith demands that our schools teach the best science, and only the best science. To teach inferior science would be stupid and, yes, irreligious.

Organizations to Contact

The editors have compiled the following list of organizations concerned with the issues debated in this book. The descriptions are derived from materials provided by the organizations. All have publications or information available for interested readers. The list was compiled on the date of publication of the present volume; the information provided here may change. Be aware that many organizations take several weeks or longer to respond to inquiries, so allow as much time as possible.

Access Research Network (ARN)
P.O. Box 38069, Colorado Springs, CO   80937-8069
(719) 633-1772
Web site: www.arn.org

ARN advocates intelligent design. ARN publishes the quarterly, peer-reviewed journal *Origins & Design* and the newsletter *ARN Announce*, recent issues of which are available on its Web site. Also on its Web site, ARN publishes *Wedge Update*, an online news column, and an elementary school science curriculum. The site also provides a searchable database and internal links to Web pages of intelligent design advocates and their publications.

American Association for the Advancement of Science (AAAS)
1200 New York Avenue NW, Washington, DC   20005
(202) 325-6440
Web site: www.aaas.org

AAAS is a nonprofit organization dedicated to advancing science around the world. It publishes *Science* magazine, recent issues of which are available on its Web site. The AAAS Web site also provides information on science topics, including evolution, and explores issues that raise religious and ethical questions, including the study guide *The Evolution Dialogues: Science, Christianity, and the Quest for Understanding.*

American Association of University Professors (AAUP)
1012 Fourteenth Street NW, Suite 500
Washington, DC   20005-3465
(202) 737-5900 • fax: (202) 737-5526
Web site: www.aaup.org

AAUP is an organization of member professors who advance academic freedom and shared governance to ensure higher education's contribution to the common good. It opposes efforts to require teachers in public schools to treat evolution as an untested hypothesis unsubstantiated by science. AAUP publishes the bimonthly magazine *Academe*, many issues of which are available on its Web site. Also on its Web site are articles on the evolution debate, including "Wedging Creationism into the Academy."

Americans United for Separation of Church and State
518 C Street NE, Washington, DC   20002
(202) 466-3234 • fax: (202) 466-2587
e-mail: americansunited@au.org
Web site: www.au.org

Americans United is a non-sectarian, non-partisan organization whose goal is to defend the separation of church and state in the courts, educate legislators, and work with media to inform Americans about issues concerning religious freedom. It opposes teaching religion, including intelligent design, in public school science classes. On its Web site, Americans United publishes fact sheets, court decision summaries, expert opinion statements on intelligent design, and the brochure *Science, Religion, and Public Education.*

Answers in Genesis (AiG)
P.O. Box 6330, Florence, KY   41022
(859) 727-2222 • fax: (859) 727-2299
Web site: www.answersingenesis.org

AiG is a creationist organization that opposes evolutionary theory because it believes in the absolute authority of the Bible as "an infallible revelation." It has built a museum in Petersburg, Kentucky, to promote its views. In 2006 AiG in America broke from AiG international, claiming it did not want to be subject to international review. The branches from Australia, Canada, New Zealand, and South Africa have renamed themselves Creation Ministries International (CMI). AiG publishes the quarterly *Answers*, the online *Journal of Biblical and Scientific Studies*, and the book *Evolution Exposed*. It publishes numerous articles on its Web site, including "Creation: Where's the Proof?"

Center for Theology and the Natural Sciences
2400 Ridge Road, Berkeley, CA   94709-1212
(510) 848-8152 • fax: (510) 848-2535
e-mail: ctnsinfo@stns.org
Web site: www.ctns.org

The center promotes the interaction between theology and modern science through research, education, and public education. It publishes books such as *CTNS/Vatican Observatory Series on Divine Action*, the tri-annual journal *Theology and Science*, and many articles, including "Theistic Evolution: A Christian Alternative to Atheism, Creationism, and Intelligent Design" and "Situating Intelligent Design in the Contemporary Debate," which are available on its Web site.

Creation Research Society (CRS)
P.O. Box 8263, St. Joseph, MO   64508-8263
e-mail: contact@creationresearch.org
Web site: www.creationresearch.org

CRS is a society of trained scientists and interested laypersons who are firmly committed to scientific creation as an alternative to evolution. Formed in 1963 by a committee of ten like-minded scientists, it has grown into an organization with worldwide membership. Its primary function is to research, develop, and test creation models. CRS publishes the *Creation Research Society Quarterly*, a peer-reviewed journal, the bi-monthly newsletter *Creation Matters*, and books, including *Science and Creation: An Introduction to Some Tough Issues*.

Creation Science Evangelism
29 Cummings Road, Pensacola, FL   32503
(850) 479-3466 • fax: (850) 479-8562
Web site: www.drdino.com

Creation Science Evangelism is the organization of Kent Hovind who calls himself "Dr. Dino." Hovind is famous for his offer to pay $250,000 to anyone who can prove evolution. He and his son hold seminars nationwide, online versions of which are available on the Web site. Numerous articles are also available on the Web site, including "Our Design Is No Accident" and "The Eyes Have It—Creation Is Reality."

Discovery Institute
1402 Third Ave., Suite 400, Seattle, WA   98101
(206) 292-0401 • fax: (206) 682-5320
e-mail: info@discovery.org
Web site: www.discovery.org

Considered the home of the intelligent design movement, the institute's stated mission is to promote representative government, the free market, and individual liberty. It publishes a monthly e-mail newsletter *Nota Bene*, which provides news and information about intelligent design issues, books such as *Darwinism, Design, and Public Education*, and reports, legislative testimony, and articles, such as "On the Origins of Life," "Intelligent Design in Biology: The Current Situation," and "Evolution and Dissent," which are available along with many other articles on its Web site.

Geoscience Research Institute (GRI)
11060 Campus Street, Loma Linda, CA   92350
(909) 558-4548 • fax: (909) 558-4314
e-mail: info@grisda.org
Web site: www.grisda.org

The Geoscience Research Institute, founded in 1958, is a Seventh-Day Adventist organization established to examine scientific evidence to refute evolutionary theory. The institute uses both science and revelation to study the question of origins because it considers the exclusive use of science too narrow an approach. GRI publishes the periodicals *Origins* and *Geoscience Reports*, recent articles from which are available on its Web site, including "Can a Scientist Also Be a Christian?" and "Do We Need to Turn Off Our Brains When We Enter a Church?"

Intelligent Design Network

P.O. Box 14702, Shawnee Mission, KS   66285-4702
(913) 268-0852
e-mail: IDnet@att.net
Web site: www.intelligentdesignnetwork.org

The Intelligent Design Network is an activist organization that seeks institutional objectivity in origins science, arguing that objectivity in the institutions of science, government, and the media will lead to good origins science and constitutional neutrality. It specifically promotes the teaching of intelligent design and criticism of evolution in schools. Its Web site publishes the network's Statement of Objectives and articles and reports, including "Intelligent Design: The Scientific Alternative to Evolution," "There Is No Conflict Between Institutionally Objective Science and Religion," and "Are We Designs or Occurrences? Should Science and Government Prejudge the Question?"

Institute for Creation Research (ICR)

10946 Woodside Ave. North, Santee, CA   92071
(619) 448-0900 • fax: (619) 448-3469

The goal of ICR is to equip believers with evidence of the Bible's accuracy and authority through scientific research and education. It publishes the monthly newsletter *Acts & Facts*, books such as *The Scientific Case Against Evolution*, and numerous articles, including "Are Sharks and People Related?" and "Creation, Corruption, and Cholera," which are available on its Web site.

National Academy of Sciences (NAS)
500 Fifth Street NW, Washington, DC   20001
(202) 334-2000
Web site: www.nasonline.org

Signed into being by President Abraham Lincoln on March 3, 1863, NAS is a society of distinguished scholars engaged in scientific and engineering research and dedicated to the use of science and technology for the general welfare. The NAS has served to "investigate, examine, experiment, and report upon any subject of science or art" whenever called upon to do so by any department of the government. Its Evolution Resources link provides access to reports, statements, and research papers, including *Science and Creationism: A View from the National Academy of Sciences.*

National Center for Science Education (NCSE)
420 Fortieth Street, Suite 2, Oakland, CA   94609-2509
(510) 601-7203 • fax: (510) 601-7204
e-mail: ncseoffice@ncseweb.org
Web site: www.natcenscied.org

The sole purpose of NCSE is to defend the teaching of evolution in public schools. The center provides information and advice for those who hope to keep evolution in the science classroom and scientific creationism out. Its Web site provides reviews of current anti-evolution activity in the United States and around the world, background information on the intelligent design movement and the creation/evolution controversy, and resources for parents, teachers, school boards, and the general public.

National Science Teachers Association (NSTA)
1840 Wilson Blvd., Arlington, VA   22201
(703) 243-7100 • fax: (703) 243-7177
Web site: www.nsta.org

NSTA is a professional association of 55,000 science teachers and administrators. In its position statement, NSTA says that it stands with other leading scientific organizations and scientists in stating that intelligent design is not science. The Evolution Resources link on its Web site provides the NSTA position statement on the teaching of evolution, a bibliography of books on evolution, and links to educational resources on evolution.

Reasons to Believe (RTB)
P.O. Box 5978, Pasadena, CA   91117
(626) 335-1480
e-mail: Feedback@reasons.org
Web site: www.reasons.org

Founded by astronomer Hugh Ross in 1986, RTB is an international, interdenominational ministry established to communicate the factual basis for belief in the Bible as the error-free Word of God. Its mission is to show that science and faith are allies, not enemies. It publishes science-specific articles in *Facts for Faith* and a quarterly review of research, *Connections*. Recent issues and archives of its publications are available on its Web site.

Bibliography

Books

Francisco J. Ayala   *Darwin's Gift to Science and Religion.* Washington, DC: Joseph Henry Press, 2007.

Randall Balmer   *Thy Kingdom Come: How the Religious Right Distorts the Faith and Threatens America.* New York: Basic Books, 2006.

Michael J. Behe   *Darwin's Black Box: The Biochemical Challenge to Evolution.* New York: Simon and Schuster, 2006.

John Brockman, ed.   *Intelligent Thought: Science versus the Intelligent Design Movement.* New York: Vintage, 2006.

John Campbell and Stephen Meyer, eds.   *Darwinism, Design, and Public Education.* East Lansing: Michigan State University Press, 2003.

William A. Dembski   *The Design Revolution: Answering the Toughest Questions about Intelligent Design.* Downers Grove, IL: InterVarsity Press, 2004.

Arri Eisen and Gary Laderman, eds.   *Science, Religion, and Society: An Encyclopedia of History, Culture, and Controversy.* Armonk, NY: M.E. Sharpe, 2007.

James H. Fetzer	*Render unto Darwin: Philosophical Aspects of the Christian Right's Crusade Against Science.* Chicago: Open Court, 2007.
Kent Greenawalt	*Does God Belong in Public Schools?* Princeton, NJ: Princeton University Press, 2005.
Guillermo Gonzalez	*The Privileged Planet: How Our Place in the Cosmos Is Designed for Discovery.* Washington, DC: Regnery, 2004.
Philip Kitcher	*Living with Darwin: Evolution, Design, and the Future of Faith.* New York: Oxford University Press, 2007.
Tim Lewens	*Darwin.* New York: Routledge, 2007.
Denyse O'Leary	*By Design or by Chance?* Minneapolis, MN: Augsburg Books, 2004.
Andrew J. Petto and Laurie R. Godfrey, eds.	*Scientists Confront Intelligent Design and Creationism.* New York: Norton, 2007.
Michael Ruse	*The Evolution-Creation Struggle.* Boston: Harvard University Press, 2005.
Michael Ruse and William A. Dembski	*Debating Design: From Darwin to DNA.* New York: Cambridge University Press, 2004.
Sahotra Sarkar	*Doubting Darwin? Creationist Designs on Evolution.* Malden, MA: Blackwell, 2007.

Niall Shanks	*God, the Devil, and Darwin: A Critique of Intelligent Design Theory.* New York: Oxford University Press, 2004.
Michael Shermer	*Science Friction: Where the Known Meets the Unknown.* New York: Times Books/Henry Holt, 2005.
Michael Shermer	*Why Darwin Matters: The Case Against Intelligent Design.* New York: Times Books/Henry Holt, 2006.
Lee Strobel	*The Case for a Creator: A Journalist Investigates Scientific Evidence that Points Toward God.* Grand Rapids, MI: Zondervan, 2004.
Jonathan Wells	*The Politically Incorrect Guide to Darwinism and Intelligent Design.* Washington, DC: Regnery, 2006.
David Sloan Wilson	*Evolution for Everyone: How Darwin's Theory Can Change the Way We Think about Our Lives.* New York: Delacorte, 2007.
Thomas Woodward and Phillip Johnson	*Doubts about Darwin: A History of Intelligent Design.* Grand Rapids, MI: Baker Book House, 2003.

Periodicals

Wayne Adkins	"Evolution Is Flawed and OJ Didn't Do It," *American Chronicle*, December 23, 2005.

Jerry Adler   "Doubting Darwin," *Newsweek*, February 7, 2005.

Stephen M. Barr   "The Miracle of Evolution," *First Things: A Monthly Journal of Religion and Public Life*, February 2006.

Celeste Biever   "Intelligent Design: The God Lab," *New Scientist*, December 15, 2006.

Patrick H. Byrne   "Evolution, Randomness, and Divine Purpose: A Reply to Cardinal Schönborn," *Theological Studies*, September 2006.

Cornelia Dean   "Opting Out in the Debate on Evolution," *New York Times*, June 21, 2005.

Cornelia Dean and Laurie Goodstein   "Leading Cardinal Redefines Church's View on Evolution," *New York Times*, July 9, 2005.

William A. Dembski   "Unintelligent Evolution," Talk Presented at the Annual American Academy of Religion Meeting, San Antonio, November 22, 2994, www.designinference.com.

Peter Dizikes   "A Real Monkey Trial," *Salon.com*, May 13, 2005.

Alexander George   "What's Wrong with Intelligent Design, and with Its Critics," *Christian Science Monitor*, December 22, 2005.

Charles C. Haynes   "Political Science: Unintelligent Debate over Intelligent Design," First Amendment Center, August 21, 2005, www.firstamendmentcenter.org.

Issues & Controversies on File	"Update: Evolution and Creationism," October 15, 2004.
Tom Junod	"The Case for Intelligent Design: It Can't Damage Science but It Will Change Christianity," *Esquire*, November 2005.
Lawrence Krauss	"School Boards Want to 'Teach the Controversy.' What Controversy?" *New York Times*, May 17, 2005.
Molleen Matsumura	"Facing Challenges to Evolution Education," National Center for Science Education. www.ncseweb.org.
Harold Morowitz, Robert Hazen, and James Trefil	"Intelligent Design Has No Place in the Science Curriculum," *Chronicle of Higher Education*, September 2, 2005.
Paul Nussbaum	"Evangelicals Divided over Evolution," *Philadelphia Enquirer*, May 30, 2005.
Michael Powell	"Doubting Rationalist: Intelligent Design Proponent Phillip Johnson, and How He Came to Be," *Washington Post*, May 15, 2005.
David Quammen	"Was Darwin Wrong?" *National Geographic*, November 2004.
Jim Remsen	"Tangling over Intelligent Design; A Biologist and a Creationist Went Head to Head in a Debate Recently over Teaching the Concept in Science Classes," *Philadelphia Inquirer*, May 29, 2005.

Robert John Russell	"Evolution and Christian Faith: A Response to Cardinal Christoph Schönborn: Intelligent Design Is an Ideology, not a Science," *America*, February 20, 2006.
Peter Slevin	"Evolution's Grass-Roots Defender Grows in Virginia," *Washington Post*, July 20, 2005.
Peter Steinfels	"Eighty Years After Scopes, A Professor Reflects on Unabated Opposition to Evolutionists," *New York Times*, June 18, 2005.
Steven Waldman	"Careful What You Wish For," *beliefnet*, 2006, www.beliefnet.com.

Web sites

Evolution Minute www.evolutionminute.com Evolution Minute posts current and archived news podcasts that feature commentary from all sides of the controversy regarding the origins of life brought about by fundamentalist Christians and Muslims questioning Charles Darwin's theory of evolution. The Web site is developed by teachers for teachers and is not affiliated with any religious or secular interest group. Its purpose is to inform and educate concerning the evolution creationism controversy.

The TalkOrigins Archive http://talkorigins.org TalkOrigins Archive is a collection of articles responding to questions posted at the talk.origins newsgroup about the debate over biological and physical origins, particularly the creation/ evolution controversy. It also posts articles rebutting assertions of intelligent design or creationist advocates.

Uncommon Descent www.uncommondescent.com Uncommon Descent is the Weblog of Intelligent Design advocates William Dembski, Denyse O'Leary, and others. Contributors believe that science is being used to promote a materialistic worldview that leads to incorrect and unsupported conclusions about biological and cosmological origins. The group argues instead that intelligent design offers a promising scientific alternative to materialistic theories and should be developed as a scientific, intellectual, and cultural project.

Index